Dad Incarnate

Dad Incarnate

Rediscovering Fatherhood

Bradford T. Stull

NOVALIS

© 2007 Novalis, Saint Paul University, Ottawa, Canada

Cover design and layout: Dominique Pelland
Cover Images: ©Ingram; ©Jupiter Images

Business Offices:
Novalis Publishing Inc.
10 Lower Spadina Avenue, Suite 400
Toronto, Ontario, Canada
M5V 2Z2

Novalis Publishing Inc.
4475 Frontenac Street
Montréal, Québec, Canada
H2H 2S2

Phone: 1-800-387-7164
Fax: 1-800-204-4140
E-mail: books@novalis.ca
www.novalis.ca

Library and Archives Canada Cataloguing in Publication

Stull, Bradford T.
    Dad incarnate : rediscovering fatherhood / Bradford T. Stull.

Includes bibliographical references.

ISBN 978-2-89507-906-4

    1. Fatherhood. I. Title.

HQ756.S785 2007   306.874'2   C2007-905102-2

Printed in Canada.

We acknowledge the financial support of the Government of Canada
through the Book Publishing Industry Development Program (BPIDP) for
our publishing activities.

5   4   3   2   1   11   10   09   08   07

To Sophie

With her, it's a whole new world.

Acknowledgments

This book emerged from a web of relationships, many of which I want to acknowledge here. Thomas Andrew Stull? He was a good man, a good father. He died young and my children and I have missed having him in our lives. Stephen H. Webb and Michael Birkel? Once again, they read what I asked them to read, selflessly and kindly. Vivian Dolkart? She witnessed the birth of this book at a very grief-filled time in my life. Kevin Burns? He remembered our long-ago meeting and remained interested in my work. Amy Heron and Anne Louise Mahoney? Editors/readers extraordinaire. Maggie, Elias and Sophie? They continue to bear loving witness to my life. What else can a husband and father need or want?

Contents

Prologue

Our Father

Our Father, who art in heaven, hallowed be thy name;
thy kingdom come; thy will be done
on earth as it is in heaven …

—The Lord's Prayer

Images
1

That night, after the Twin Towers fell, after part of the
Pentagon lay burning, after that lonely Pennsylvania field ex-
ploded into flame, I found myself invoking a prayer I hadn't
said in years. It was a prayer I had learned as a child, a prayer
that Jesus—and my own parents and church—had taught me
to pray. I had put the prayer away because I didn't believe it.
I didn't believe it, because I didn't believe that God was father,
or father alone. I didn't believe it, because I didn't believe that

there was or is a kingdom to come. After all, if I rejected the metaphorical "gender-fication" of God as father, I had to reject the vision of a kingdom. What else is a king but the father of a realm? I had found myself as a religion major, as a seminary student, wondering about the possibility of a commonwealth in which not King, but Love, is the binding force of community.

Still, I found myself that night in the darkness of my bedroom falling asleep with the Lord's Prayer on my lips. The psychic turmoil brought on by 9/11 brought back the prayer I thought I had left behind. The angst born from 9/11 has faded, but its effect has remained. Even as anxieties come and go, the prayer remains.

Images
2

As the young couple—she in her white gown, he in his black tuxedo—sat on their chairs at the top of the chancel, immediately in front of the long, broad table on which the death and resurrection of Jesus would be ritualistically recast into the bread and wine of the Last Supper and then shared with the gathered, I looked at my niece with a certain wonder. She was a grown woman, she whom I had carried as a mewling baby, trying to comfort her. She had converted to Roman Catholicism at 16, with her bemused (if confused) mother, father, brother and sisters looking on. They belonged to no organized religion, and her father in particular had no use for church. Still, she con-

verted, searching for and seemingly finding a religious home. And so, here I was: present to witness this marriage, a marriage consecrated not only by her father from whose loins she had sprung, but also by a father in robes and the father God of the prayer that Jesus taught us to pray, a prayer the robed priest invited the gathered to say together.

◎　　◎　　◎

Our Father, Omnipresent and Yet ...

"Our Father" refers to the God of the Lord's Prayer, but also cannot help but call to mind the men who share with Jesus' God the moniker and position of father—biological, adoptive or religious. Precisely because these fathers have been interlinked for millennia, it is not easy to speak of one type of father without invoking, however obliquely, the other, for good or for bad. Such is the connotative web that any word weaves.

Consider, for instance, Martin Luther King's brilliant discussion of the word *blackness*.[1] It connotes not only the colour black but also such words as *night*, *fear* and *evil*. When people in the Americas who are of African descent are called "blacks," King's words remind us that this web of connotations immediately converges, often to the detriment of the people in question. So it is with *father*—at least in the West. *Father*, for many, involves both God and earthly fathers, and all the images, feelings, thoughts and desires that accompany that word.

That there are negative connotations is the point that feminist theologians and feminist biblical scholars have been making ever since Mary Daly launched her justly famous and infamous book, *Beyond God the Father* (Daly, 1973). In that book, Daly challenges us to reconceive the father God in terms other than male. Why? Because intoning God as father leads us to make fathers—and thus all males—into gods. God cannot be father, Daly argues, without fathers and men being gods. The result, plain and simple, is a sexist, misogynistic social order in which women are systematically oppressed. As Daly maintains early in the book, "Sexual caste is hidden by ideologies that bestow false identities upon women and men. Patriarchal religion has served to perpetuate all these dynamics of delusion, naming them as 'natural' and bestowing its supernatural blessings upon them" (Daly, 1973, p. 3). Borrowing from understandings of caste in traditional Indian society, with its strict delineation at the extremes between Brahmans and untouchables, Daly suggests that Western gender division has likewise been ordered. Men are the Brahmans, the caste of power and prestige. Women are the untouchables, simultaneously necessary to maintain the social order and outside the circles of power and prestige. These are our identities: men as the centre of power; women as powerless, servants to those in power.

For Daly, needless to say, these identities are false: they are oppressive creations that enable men and disable women. Supporting these false identities, however, is a very powerful symbol system: patriarchal religion. To wit: if God is understood as father (and thus male), fathers (and thus, by extension, all men) are understood to be uniquely godlike.

In Daly's view, since women do not have a corresponding link to the divine order, they are understood to be uniquely not godlike. When humans imagine God as father and thus male, she argues, they see earthly fathers and thus males as the natural heirs of God's power, natural extensions of God's being in the world. Women are understood to be subordinate, naturally, to these godlike beings: fathers and men.

Daly develops her argument in this way: "The symbol of the Father God, spawned in the human imagination and sustained as plausible by patriarchy, has in turn rendered service to this type of society by making its mechanisms for the oppression of women appear right and fitting" (Daly, 1973, p. 13). Three points are crucial: father God is a symbol; this symbol is sustained by patriarchy; and patriarchy uses this symbol to create and maintain a society in which the oppression of women is seen as "right and fitting."

With regard to the first point, Daly realizes that when we speak of God as father, we speak symbolically, or, more precisely, metaphorically. I will develop this idea more fully in chapter 1, but for now let us grant Daly her point: all talk of God is imaginative, the result of humans attempting to name the divine beyond and within themselves.

Regarding the second and third points, Daly has concluded that in a patriarchal society, men use the image of the father God to keep themselves at the apex of power. Most humans love and crave power, and men are no different. When they have God in their corner, so to speak, why would they give up power, unless they have undergone profound spiritual change and want to share power throughout the social order? Daly is skeptical about fathers and men wanting to share power. In her own professional and personal experience, men will not and cannot reimagine God and themselves, because they love power and love to lord it over women.

Daly's heirs extend her original work, albeit with some differences. Rosemary Radford Ruether, Elizabeth Schüssler Fiorenza, Sallie McFague, Patricia Wilson Kastner, Sr. Anne Carr and Rebecca Chopp, to name a few luminaries in this herstory, brilliantly bring the insights of feminist theory and practice to bear on theology and religious life.

McFague, for example, argues that our image of God as father, as with all metaphors that serve as models, has become "reified, petrified, and expanded so as not only to exclude other models but also to pretend to the status of definitions" (McFague, 1987, p. 39). We come to think that this metaphor is not a metaphor but, rather, a fact. God *is* father; God *is* male. If this model is a factual description of divine reality, then it is difficult for earthly fathers and all men to refrain from holding themselves up as the apex of power, as the highest caste. If, however, and this is McFague's point, we understand that our image of God as father is a metaphor, then we realize it is tentative, experimental, even transitory.

As we begin our exploration of the place and possibility of fatherhood in the 21st century, we need to take feminist theology and feminist biblical studies seriously; we need to honour their insights, which here I boil down to two.

First, if we reify our image of God as father, if we allow it to become a fact, we move into dangerous ground in which earthly fathers can easily be seen, as Daly argues, as the Brahmans in a society in which mothers, women and even girls are objects of oppression.

Second, if we remember, as McFague argues, that metaphors are experiments—tentative symbols of that which cannot be finally named or fully understood—then a world of imagining opens to us. This is a world in which we are less sure of the ways things are and should be, a world in which we can work toward what Daly considers to be the human imperative. "To exist humanly," she writes, "is to name the self, the world, and God" (Daly, 1973, p. 8).

In short, Daly holds that we are not fully human until we can name reality, free of the oppression of others naming it for us. All humans ask this fundamental question: Who am I? Daly asserts that we all have the right and responsibility to answer that question for ourselves, not to have another answer it for us. The same holds for these questions: What is the world? What is God? This is not to say that we should accept the easy, sloppy relativism invoked by the phrase "I'm O.K., you're O.K." We do, after all, live in community and must be in conversation with our past and present, our family, our friends, even strangers. Yet, as Daly claims, if we are to be fully human we cannot and should not allow our questions to be answered only by others. The result, according to the feminist critique of God as father, is misogyny.

We have all suffered under a misogynistic social order supported by, and supportive of, misogynistic religious practices. Understanding God as father solely and uniquely has allowed us to understand fathers as gods, with often disastrous results. For example, only fathers who understand themselves as gods—of a certain sort—can justify the abuse they visit upon their children and spouses. Just as in certain biblical stories God the father smites his children's enemies and indeed even his children, fathers as gods smite their children and their children's enemies. Simply put, God the father too often has been understood to be vengeful and violent, and fathers as gods have acted likewise, often toward their own families.

Fathers of families are not the only culprits. If medieval popes and kings were the fathers of their peoples—ordained in their positions by divine right—we would have been better off without such fathers. These fathers forced conversion to Roman Catholicism at the points of swords and the tips of flames; launched bloody crusades upon the "infidels" of other faiths; and justified an oppressive social order marked by serfs at the bottom and nobility at the top as the order that best represented God's divine will. Even a cursory examination of the history of the link between God the father and fathers as gods reveals that there is, indeed, a problem.

Father is a word fraught with difficulty. For many people, the word connotes the abusive, destructive father, earthly and divine. Thus, one is tempted to let go of this word for God. If, following feminist theology, we can rethink God as something other than father, we can rethink fathers as something other than gods. For that matter, we can think of fathers as something other than fathers, if, indeed, we see fathers as Brahmans who are willing to oppress the untouchables and other lesser castes.

Coincident to the rise of feminism has been a crisis in fatherhood. This is not to say that feminist theory and practice has caused this crisis. Rather, as we have engaged in a powerful conversation about men and women in general, and about the way we envision God in particular, fatherhood—as we name it and practise it—has reached a crossroads.

That said, *father* also connotes safety, care, love, happiness and hope. Indeed, the first image at the opening of this prologue shows that I sought these very things when I returned to the Lord's Prayer. When evil and tragedy beset my psyche, I looked to the father God for help, for assurance, for comfort. When the young couple of the second image marry with the blessings of the father God, the father priest and their earthly, biological fathers, they do so with the expectation that blessings will contribute to a fruitful life together, a life marked by joy, happiness and love. When a child stubs his toe and asks his father for a kiss and a Band-Aid, he expects to receive kindness and help. When a child is afraid and runs to her father for safety, she expects to find it. Certainly Jesus, that radical messenger of radical love, saw his father God as the source of such love.

Father thus connotes God and human, bad and good, but it also connotes failure.

This failing has been a long time coming. However, come it has. We can either ignore the crisis and let it continue, or we can confront it in all its extraordinary complexity—theoretical and practical, symbolic and material—in the hope of understanding it, stopping it and correcting it. Three choices lie before us. We can throw the idea of father away. We can muddle along with it as it is, and suffer as a result. Or we can rethink it, reclaim it and renew it.

This book contends that it is on the theoretical and symbolic levels—the level of metaphor—that we must earnestly confront the crisis, because it is the theories and symbols that name and support how we practise fatherhood. We will find ourselves rethinking what we mean by *father* and *fatherhood* in ways that for now we can only glimpse. In the end, we must engage in conversation with the deepest strands of feminism and, at the same time, create a new place for fathers and fatherhood—biological, adoptive, religious, divine—alongside mothers and motherhood.

One cannot simply rethink earthly fathers and fatherhood without also rethinking the divine fatherhood of God. While this book is not meant to be a study of the theology of God's fatherhood, the book intentionally speaks to fathers and fatherhood writ large. Thus, it is appropriate to begin with a discussion of the prayer that Jesus taught us to pray.

Why? Because we live in a culture whose fathers are named by the visions and tensions at play in Lord's Prayer. To understand that fatherhood is in crisis, and that we need to search for a metaphor that helps name and engender fathers as liberating agents in the lives of their children and, indeed, of the mothers of those children, we must understand the ways in which "Our Father" is part of the North American cultural narrative's deepest weave.

Each week, millions of Christian faithful—and not so faithful—say the Lord's Prayer at church services: Roman Catholic, Southern Baptist, Anglican, Disciples of Christ,

Presbyterian, Methodist, Pentecostal—you name it. The prayer is also prayed at funerals, weddings and other formal rituals that fall outside the bounds of normal weekly worship, making culture's deepest foundations. Moreover, the prayer finds utterance in tens of millions of private moments—moments of grief, joy, terror, confusion and angst.

One wonders how many times, in the private moments of their own lives, people prayed this prayer in the days and weeks following 9/11. Even those who don't consciously believe in or imagine God as father undoubtedly found comfort in this prayer and the order that it apparently offers: a father God who is king and who can provide bread, forgive sins, keep people from temptation and, most importantly, deliver people from evil. Is this not what all children want: a father who, in the face of horrific evil, can protect and save them? In our deepest moments of trouble, do we not look to the father God—indeed *the* father—as the deliverer, the "everlasting arms," in the words of Deuteronomy 33:27, in which we can find comfort?

These words are echoed in the poem "Suspended," by Anglo-American poet Denise Levertov. She writes,

> The 'everlasting arms' my sister loved
>   to remember
> must have upheld my leaden weight
> from falling, even so
> (Levertov, 1997, p. 24)

Levertov names wonderfully what it is that all children want from their fathers: strong arms that will stop them from a free fall into what lies below. This is one of the poles of our understanding of *father*: he is a protector and defender, an all-embracing, all-enveloping presence. Even more, we seek a father who will stop us from a free fall even when we do not realize that he is holding us up. We want freedom, and yet we want protection. Levertov reminds us that we can't see those arms that must be there. The speaker of the poem knows that she or he is being held up, but feels "nothing, no embrace." God as the everlasting arms is simultaneously present and absent.

This poem helps us understand in a new way the prayer that Jesus taught us. Why did he metaphorically name God as father? One self-evident reason is this: fundamental to human experience is the desire for a father who is protector, deliverer and forgiver, a father who justly orders our existence, a father who keeps our leaden weight from falling deep into the abyss. However, Jesus' prayer also names the fundamental problems of the father in our culture. The negative metaphors about father and fatherhood that resound in the North American cultural narrative—father as distant, all-powerful, other—are present both explicitly and implicitly in the prayer.

The father God of the Lord's Prayer is a distant lawgiver. Even if his kingdom comes, the father God remains apart. This, to be sure, is the vision presented by C.S. Lewis in his delightful and magisterial classic *The Lion, the Witch, and the Wardrobe*. The Emperor over the Sea—symbolically, God the father—writes the "deep magic" into creation, but is never fully, materially present in Narnia. Only Aslan, his avatar, his messenger—indeed, his son, the Christ figure—

appears in that land. The Emperor is a distant if benevolent lawgiver, a father king, who promises order and protection but who is wholly other.

The Gospels (Matthew 6:9-13; Luke 11:2-4) present the Lord's Prayer in two ways, and these have their own variants, depending on the church. One of the best known is the following:

Our Father, who art in heaven, hallowed be thy name;
thy kingdom come; thy will be done
on earth as it is in heaven.
Give us this day our daily bread;
and forgive us our trespasses,
as we forgive those who trespass against us;
and lead us not into temptation,
but deliver us from evil.
For thine is the kingdom, and the power, and the glory,
for ever and ever. Amen.

Much has been written on this prayer. This prologue aims not to rehearse or even study what has already been said but rather to explore what this prayer means for our understanding of father: how this prayer, in its omnipresent incantatory power, reveals the omnipresence and omniabsence of fathers and our desire for them in this presence/absence.

The first line of the prayer immediately suggests to us the depth and extent of the issue: we pray to the father God, but he is elsewhere, and not just anywhere, but in heaven. On the one hand, this is beneficial: the father God to whom we pray is where we all hope to be after we die. On the other hand, father God's place in heaven is troubling: why isn't he here, helping us in the flesh? To be sure, Christianity answers that question in its claim that Jesus, who lived among us as a human being, is God incarnate. But recall where the prayer appears in the gospel narratives. It is prior to Passover; Jesus has yet to be proclaimed as Christ crucified and resurrected. Also, remember that Jesus is directing his followers' attentions not to himself but to another, to the father God who is in heaven and who can, the remainder of the prayer suggests, help us in our time of need. Even as the Gospels tell us that Jesus is the son of God with whom God is "well pleased" (Matthew 3:17), Jesus does not point to himself as the father. As Aslan does, Jesus looks to the "Emperor over the Sea."

Yet the prayer also suggests that this division is not eternal. Jesus teaches us to hope for a time in which earth mirrors heaven: we want father God's kingdom to come to us, the earth to become as heaven. Jesus, indeed, is not an escapist, looking to a better life beyond earth. He wants God's rule to be earth's rule; he wants the line between heaven and earth to be permeable. A central feature of this rule, of this "magic," to invoke Lewis's image, is this: "forgive us our trespasses [sins] as we forgive those who trespass [sin] against us." This is an image of humility, of harmony. Jesus recognizes that we make mistakes, but that father God can forgive us of these mistakes. Moreover, and this is the radical vision of Jesus' prayer, we can forgive each other, as father God can forgive us. Indeed, we should forgive each other. We are not trapped in a world of revenge, oppressive power, animosity and hatred when we take seriously our relationship to our father God. We can, indeed, act like the father, offering forgiveness to each other. What is the point of forgiveness? To establish and re-establish harmony, to reach out to each other, to embrace each other. We are not called to stand as damning judges. We are not called to condemn each other for our transgressions, throwing each other into the literal and metaphoric abysses of death and violence. Rather, we are called to another way of being.

The remainder of this book explores what this new way of being might mean for earthly fathers, and thereby obliquely suggests how we might begin to reconsider all fathers, earthly and divine. What is it for them to enter another way of being? To ask for forgiveness and to forgive? To stand not as judges, not as condemners, not as distant gods who proclaim law and judgment, but as fathers wishing to enter into the lives of their children and establish harmony, so that a new image of being can emerge? Before we can answer these questions, there is a long story to tell: a story about deadbeats, thundergods, architects, fools, and Mr. Moms.

1

The Universe of Metaphor

◎   ◎   ◎

Images

1

With which image should this book begin?

Perhaps with an early day in my son's life.

I remember clearly that dim first night when he cried from his own room, not soon after my wife and I had created it for him and him alone. Alone. He was alone, although we—his mother and father—slept together.

For the first few weeks of his life, of course, he slept in our room, in a handmade wooden drop cradle. A friend of ours, a Quaker carpenter, had made it out of cherry wood. It was simple, exquisitely so. Our friend's own daughter had slept in it as a babe, had warmed it with her own self. My son was happy to sleep in it, next to my side of the bed. He slept next to me so that my wife might have some respite from the trauma of a C-section and the demands of breastfeeding. If my son woke not to eat, not to have his diaper changed, but simply to cry out in existential desire and need, I would rock him back to sleep. I wouldn't get out of bed—not my whole body, at least. I would just stick out my right leg, foot extended, and gently rock the cradle. With luck, by grace, my son would sleep again, assured that he was not alone, that the movement from womb to world had not left him bereft, without anchor, floating in the tempest of life.

As soon as we thought it feasible, we moved him to his own room. Having left the womb, he also left our presence at night. He would wake, however, crying to nurse, to be changed, but also painfully and angst-fully.

So it was at 3 a.m. that night. He was not crying from hunger; he had eaten 20 minutes before. He was not crying because his diaper needed to be changed; he was dry. He cried, rather, to be held, and to be assured that he was not alone, that he had, in a word, family.

I went to him. This was my job, as the one who couldn't breastfeed, who was not at home during the day. Early on that Indiana morning, I held this baby who was my son, this son who was my first child and who looked like a little old man. I picked him up, held him against my chest and neck, one hand on his diapered bottom, the other holding his back and head. I walked, I cooed, I swayed, I thought (or, at least, felt; the thoughts came later, over the next days as I ruminated on this experience):

I have no clue what I'm doing. I have no models, no memory of my own father comforting me, no sense of other fathers ever comforting an infant, ever cradling it in their arms, next to their breast, as if... as if... as if... they were a mother.

◎   ◎   ◎

Images
2

With which image should this book begin?

Perhaps with the image of my own father at his father's funeral.

My paternal grandfather was a World War I veteran; hence, his coffin was draped in an American flag. Before the coffin was lowered into the ground, the honour guard—men from the area Veterans of Foreign Wars organization and the American Legion, old soldiers all—removed the flag and folded it into a tight triangle. They handed it to my father—an Air Force veteran—for he was the "blood" of this man newly dead; the eldest son—who had served on the battlefields of Germany in World War II—was not a blood son. My own father in turn gave the flag to his nephew—himself a veteran of the jungles of Vietnam—because this nephew had loved and cared for the man now in the ground. Observing the proceedings, I cried for my uncle who was not given the flag. I cried for my father who was and who passed it on. I cried for my cousin who received it gratefully, tenderly.

Following the ceremony, I realized that my own father had not shed one tear during it all. His father had returned to dust and he had not cried.

"Why?"

"It's hard to cry for a man you hated."

My father had done his duty, but had not felt it: the wounds were too deep, too old, too close to the surface, too new.

◎　　◎　　◎

Images
3

With which image should this book begin?

Perhaps with the image of a good friend who had freedom. Freedom to choose to work half time so that he could be present for his children. Freedom for fatherhood.

His wife, a physician, was compelled by personal desire and market forces beyond her control to work nearly full time. If she wanted to work outside the home—which she did—she had to work what she could negotiate. So she did. So her husband did not. He arranged his own career as a college professor to meet the rhythms of their family.

It was not a courageous choice for him, economically. They lived simply and thus were able to choose not to be a full-fledged dual-income family. Moreover, his wife's income as a physician—albeit a public health physician—combined with his own salary made them more than comfortable. It was not a courageous choice for him, personally. Other men might feel emasculated by a life in which they change diapers more than their wives do, in which they cook for the family more than their wives do, in which they tote a child around more than their wives do, but he didn't. If he thought about masculinity, he thought about it in terms counter to the dominant images in North American culture. His own masculinity—manifest in part in his fatherhood—found power in his choice to be something of what our culture awkwardly, but sweetly, calls a stay-at-home dad. His choice to forgo a full-time career for a particular version of fatherhood was born of his own desire to be present, to attend, to respond to the call of his wife and his daughter.

Images
4

With which image should this book begin?

Perhaps with the image of a father whom I don't know or, rather, know only through a simple newspaper report.

Bizarrely, tragically, horribly (as if yet one more adverb could describe this act adequately), a young mother stabbed her children.

Why?

She was upset. Her children, ages 10 and 13, had, according to her, damaged some stuffed animals that were dear to her. As if the children were too powerful, too rebellious, for the mother to deal with alone, she enlisted an accomplice.

Who?

Her husband: the father of these children.

He held them while she stabbed them. They lived, but certainly will live with visions not only of a mother who penetrated their tender flesh with a knife but also of a father who helped her, sided with her against them.

Images
5

With which image should this book begin?

Perhaps with the image of me looking at a picture to the right of the computer on which I am writing this sentence.

The photograph shows my son and daughter snuggled up together under the bedcovers, only two months after my daughter was born. He is smiling delightedly; she is open mouthed, open eyed, open souled. I look at the picture, as I always do, and energy spreads through my entire body. I'm stunned, I'm amazed, I'm grateful that these children have come into my life. While I know the biology of childbirth, I also know that they came by acts of grace, gifts both. No longer do I wonder how to comfort either: my awkwardness of care that revealed itself in the first few months of my son's life has passed as I have learned from my wife, from myself, from my children.

Images
6

With which image should this book begin?

Perhaps with the image of an estranged wife and husband sitting across the table from each other at their son's school, talking with a school counsellor, a school psychologist and a teacher, about their son.

The boy is in trouble because he is in pain from the chaos of his family life, a life broken by his father, who left him and his brothers and his mother for another woman and another life. The father has little contact with the son and offers little financial support to the mother. As a result, she has to work 12- to 16-hour days to pay her mortgage. The school psychologist asks her how long she will need to continue working such long hours. Certainly, her absence is only compounding her son's trouble. In frustration, out of anger, the mother turns on her estranged husband, her son's estranged father, and declares that if he would help with the mortgage she wouldn't have to work so much. He sits, impassive. Finally, he offers help, of a sort: he might be able to take his son an evening or two a week.

With which image should this book begin?

Perhaps none.

One might ask, after all, why begin with any image? Why not begin with history, anthropology, sociology, biology, psychology, theology? After all, the word *father* and, indeed, the practice of fatherhood have histories and can be understood historically. So, too, the word *father* and the practice of fatherhood have anthropologies and can be understood anthropologically. Sociologically. Biologically. Psychologically. Theologically.

However, this book is not a history of fatherhood, nor is it anthropology, sociology, biology, psychology or theology. Rather, it is a study of the metaphors of fatherhood present in the North American cultural narrative, which is the intertwined collections of stories that North America tells about itself in various forms—films, novels, short stories, poems, advertisements and television shows among them. These stories are drawn from a range of times and, indeed, from beyond North America itself. Often, stories from 150 years ago demonstrate just how deep and pervasive our metaphors are. North America was not born ex-nihilo (from nothing), but rather from something. One of the great shadows is, of course, Britain. Thus, we can discover who we are through what were British stories originally. George Eliot, for instance, is as much part of the North American cultural narrative as Flannery O'Connor. As North Americans we continue to read Eliot's novels for entertainment, for enlightenment. On one extreme, we have fathers presented as deadbeat dads. On the other extreme, we have fathers presented as Mr. Mom. Between these extremes, three other negative metaphors for fathers dominate the cultural narrative: father as thundergod, father as architect and father as fool.

In one way, these metaphors help us to understand who fathers are and might become. In the case of the pedophile and the deadbeat, we are able to name diseases that afflict families. In the case of the thundergod, architect and fool, we are able to see typical and stereotypical representations of fathers that inhabit our lives in addition to our narratives. These metaphors bring into bold relief the problems inherent in them. In the case of Mr. Mom, we see a hopeful phenomenon: fathers who are moving deeply and fully into their children's lives.

Although our stories have good reason to confer these names on fathers, these metaphors are inadequate because they do not and cannot serve as agents of liberation for fathers and for all those whom fathers affect. What does *liberation* mean? Why is it the criterion for judging? For now, we can say that this book assumes that liberation is central to the human trajectory. If fathers are meant to do anything, they are meant to help their children, and thereby themselves and their spouses and partners, become more fully human, more fully liberated.

Metaphors and World Views

History, anthropology, sociology, biology, psychology and theology have all offered salient critiques of the problem of fatherhood. What has not been adequately explored, much to our detriment, is the play of metaphors for father that work to name and shape who fathers are and who fathers might become.

Why is this play of metaphors important?

It is important because the metaphors our cultural narrative offers name the problems and suggest alternatives. In so doing, metaphors shape our thinking about fathers and fatherhood. In short, metaphors reveal, inform, challenge and sustain world views. Anyone who remembers his or her own childhood or who has raised or is raising children knows this, at least implicitly. When children play, they often play within fantastic worlds that are fully realized metaphorical extensions of reality. Any doll, for instance— be it a baby doll or an action figure—is a metaphor. Is the baby doll really a baby? No. As metaphors, dolls allow children—girls and boys—to explore what they aren't but most likely will become: parents. When my daughter says she is the mommy of one of her dolls, she enters into a fantastical, metaphorical world in which literal identities are transformed into metaphorical identities. The doll is not a doll but her baby, whom she changes, feeds, rocks, cuddles and cares for. She is not a four-year-old but a mommy, who has given birth to and now is raising a baby.

Another way to think about the importance and power of metaphors in shaping our world views is to consider the theory of symbolic interactionism, as developed by George Herbert Mead and summarized by Julia T. Wood. According to Wood, "symbolic interactionism ... holds that individuals learn to participate competently in their society and to share its values through communication (symbolic interaction) with others ... awareness of personal identity arises out of communication with others who pass on the values and expectations of a society" (Wood, 2003, p. 52). As symbols, metaphors mediate the complex relationships that people have with the social order. These symbols challenge us, cajole us and nurture us. In short, they *inform* us, helping to make us who we are by entering into and shaping our selves.

The power of metaphor in our lives became exceptionally clear to me when we, as a family, watched (and watched and watched and watched and watched) *The Incredibles*, the winner of the 2005 Academy Award for best animated feature. The film centres on a family of five. The father and mother are "supers" (short for superheroes) in hiding; North American society has rejected them and other supers for being too extraordinary. The children—teenage daughter, preadolescent son and baby—all have superpowers as well. By the end of the film, the family has worked to defeat the bad guy and is prepared to go into action again when needed.

My then four-year-old daughter made it clear to us that this movie spoke to her and that she had made a metaphor of our family to allow this movie to enter into her play world. Who am I as the father? Mr. Incredible. My wife? Elastigirl. My son? Dash. My daughter? Violet. Since we do not have an infant, one of my daughter's baby dolls plays the role of Jack-Jack.

The Incredibles are complicated metaphors. They stand for the good, the true and the just, to be sure. But they also stand for other dynamics. One? Middle-aged male feelings of inadequacy: Mr. Incredible, as Bob Parr, works as a beat-en-down insurance adjuster still longing for his days as Mr. Incredible. Another? Elastigirl, Helen Parr, is a housewife trying to be normal, trying to cope with a depressed hus-band who ignores her and their children—a teenage daugh-ter full of angst, a son who wants to compete in sports but isn't allowed to because of his superpowers, and an infant who seems not to have any superpowers at all.

When my daughter imagines us as The Incredibles, she is responding to the extraordinary power of metaphor to help us try on roles, to help name who we are and who we might become. I can't imagine that she is fully aware of what she offers to us. If I take her playing seriously, I am asked to confront, in the deepest part of me, a profound question. To me, a middle-aged father who spends his days writing, read-ing, teaching and playing with his children, she offers me the opportunity to see myself as what I am certainly not: an animated superhero torn by middle-aged angst. Along with Mr. Incredible, I am forced to ask myself whether I have treated my family as if they were my greatest adventure. Or have I ignored them and who they are, dreaming of other adventures that don't include them?

Christians and other religious folk have long understood the power of metaphor to name who we are and might become. When Christians, for instance, are asked to take up their crosses, they are asked to take on the role of Jesus walking toward Golgotha. Are Christians really Jesus? Of course not. However, their tradition demands that they become, metaphorically, children of God, willing to follow the way of God the father even unto death. Zen Buddhists are told in a famous koan, if you meet the Buddha in the road, kill him. In other words, they are enjoined not to be trapped by the false metaphors that seek to ensnare them, that seek to present an illusion instead of what really is. This rejection of the false Buddha does not deny that metaphors are powerful. On the contrary, it reminds Zen Buddhists that metaphors are extremely powerful, that they create realities, and that they name who we are and who we might become.

To say that this book is a study of fatherhood from the perspective of metaphor is itself a metaphor. Metaphor, in and of itself, does not have a perspective. To suggest that it does is to personify the word: to give it vision, if not consciousness. Can metaphor have vision? No. Consciousness? No. *Metaphor*, literally, is a term that names a linguistic and thus conceptual phenomenon.[2]

Many readers likely remember this definition given to them by their teachers: a metaphor is the comparison of two things without using the words *like* or *as*. My son's fifth-grade classmates knew this definition well enough to recite it when asked, and it is a good working definition. Metaphor's partner, simile, is the comparison of two things using *like* or *as*. Here is an example of metaphor: that father is a devil. Here is an example of simile: that father is like a devil.

One drawback to this classroom definition is that it makes metaphor the negative image of simile. Simile emerges as the standard by which metaphor is judged. Metaphor, however, is much more than simile's negative image; it is even more than comparison. It is, in a fundamental way, as Kenneth Burke, one of the germinal language theorists of the last century, would say, "identification" (Burke, 1968, p. 503).

The key word in the phrase "that father is a devil" is the copula *is*, which makes a claim about the equivalency of being. Roughly speaking, one can think of *is* mathematically: it simply compares *father* and *devil*. Certainly, a comparison occurred prior to the formation of the sentence. One has to see in the father characteristics that he shares with a devil. Once the metaphor is launched, however, the comparison gives way to identification: the father is—the father equals—a devil. This discussion of identification is important because, as we shall see, metaphors are part of the construction and maintenance of world views.

Burke suggests that we define *metaphor* as follows: "a device for seeing something in terms of something else" (Burke, 1968, p. 503).

Following after Burke, George Lakoff and Mark Johnson also hold that "the essence of metaphor is understanding and experiencing one kind of thing in terms of another" (Lakoff and Johnson, 2003, p. 5).[3] Key to both Burke's and Lakoff and Johnson's definitions is the phrase *in terms of*.

We could say that A is B in order to understand B in terms of A. For instance, a daughter might describe her beloved late father as "a beacon in my troubled life." He was not literally a beacon, but metaphorically, he was, at least in his daughter's eyes. In order to make sense of her father and her experience of him, she speaks of him, and understands him, in terms of something that he literally was not: a beacon. He was not *like* a beacon; he was not *as* a beacon. He *was* a beacon: his identity merged with that light source.

Metaphor has often been denigrated as the province of poets and novelists, as if it belongs to them and them alone. As Lakoff and Johnson write, "Metaphor is for most people a device of the poetic imagination and the rhetorical flourish—a matter of extraordinary rather than ordinary language" (Lakoff and Johnson, 2003, p. 3). Nothing could be further from the truth. Metaphor is fundamental to human language, wherever it is used, whoever is using it. To be sure, Lakoff and Johnson go further. They maintain that metaphor is also fundamental to thought and action. I will develop this thread in greater detail below, when the discussion turns to world views. For now we can say that Lakoff and Johnson, like Burke before them, understand that metaphor is everywhere: it permeates human life.

The sports pages of any newspaper demonstrate this truth. Consider, for instance, a *Nashua Telegraph* headline about the Boston Red Sox arranging for the players to receive their World Series rings at the 2005 home opener, against none other than the New York Yankees. The headline reads "Opening circus to include Sox' rings." Will it be a literal circus? No, unless the Red Sox turn beloved

Fenway Park into a big top moments before the first pitch is delivered. Obviously, the headline is metaphorical. It is trying to reveal what the atmosphere of the game might be. The season before, the Red Sox had won their first World Series in 86 years. To do so, they came back from a 3–0 American League Championship Series deficit to win the series 4–3. Whom did they beat? Their arch-nemesis, the Yankees. The atmosphere at the home opener promises to be a circus: any Yankees–Red Sox game is high drama and, to add insult to injury, the Red Sox will receive their rings as the Yankees watch, waiting to play the team that beat them. Of course, the circus metaphor permeates culture. "How was the party?" It was a circus. "How was the class?" It was a circus. "How was the store?" It was a circus.

The names of sports teams themselves are almost always metaphors. Are the Indianapolis Colts literally colts? Are the Boston Red Sox literally red socks? Are the Purdue Boilermakers literally boilermakers? Are the Toronto Maple Leafs literally maple leaves? Of course, one might say that the sports pages of newspapers are poetic or rhetorical: they exist on the extremes of language use. To say that the newspaper sports pages use metaphor is not to prove, necessarily, that metaphor is fundamental to human language.

Consider, then, a sentence taken from an advertisement at a café. On each table stands a three-dimensional triangle about eight inches high by five inches wide. It advertises various breads, salads and sandwiches. As part of the side of the triangle on which chicken is advertised, this question leads the paragraph: "What's the key to tender, flavourful chicken?" The word *key* is the key to the metaphor. It suggests that tender, flavourful chicken is locked away, a treasure waiting to be discovered. If one has the key, one can access, recover and eat this treasure. Is there a literal key involved in cooking chicken? Only the key to the kitchen. Literally, cooking chicken requires no key. Metaphorically, it might.

Or, consider the phrase *I really got into that music*. The verb phrase, *got into*, is fundamentally metaphorical. The preposition, *into*, combined with the verb, *got*, suggests that the subject is able to move from the space where he or she is to another space entirely. This space, the music, is enclosed. It is the sort of space that one can move in to. To say "in" is to suggest "out." If one gets into music, one is leaving the space outside of music to the space of music itself, which is in, wherever that might be.

Even if one grants that metaphor is fundamental to human language, that it belongs to all of us, and not just to poets and novelists (and sportswriters), one might also say that metaphor is the act of adornment. We use it to add a flower to the top of the cake, to embellish our music with one more chord, to decorate our house with one more colour of paint. Metaphor is not fundamental to structure, be it a cake, a musical composition or a house. It is an addition—one that often appears to obfuscate the truth. Hence, we have the phrases *mere rhetoric* or *that was just rhetoric*. Metaphor, part of the study of rhetoric since Aristotle, is condemned by these phrases. They suggest that what the politician is saying can be divided into two categories: substance and style. If only one could cut away the style, one could discover the substance.

For example, consider the comment made by a National Public Radio newsreader on March 21, 2005. She and a reporter were discussing a decision by Israel to continue to build 3,500 homes in a West Bank settlement contiguous with Jerusalem. The reporter said that a "Palestinian negotiator" claimed that if Israel built these homes—thus solidifying Israel's territorial hold on Jerusalem—it would mean the "end of the peace process." The newsreader remarked that she wasn't sure whether the Palestinian negotiator's remark was "just rhetoric." The Palestinian negotiator had spoken of the peace process, indicating that peace could be achieved through a process that had a potential end. In other words, it is a temporal and spatial activity, limited by time and space. The newsreader questioned the negotiator's literal sincerity. That is to say, she distinguished between form and content, style and substance. She was allowing that the negotiator's metaphor might have been a fiction devised to elicit a response from Israel. In short, it might have been hyperbole: an extraordinary exaggeration meant to fool or trick Israel into reversing its decision.

Of course, US presidential candidates (and indeed all candidates for public office) are often accused of spouting rhetoric or using inflammatory rhetoric. Such criticisms are themselves metaphoric. To say that one "spouts" is to speak of the action of a whale, a fountain, a water hose: the powerful, forceful spray of a liquid into the air. To say that one's language is inflammatory is to speak of flames, combustion, fiery chaos. These phrases demonstrate the point: metaphor is not mere adornment. To criticize the use of metaphor by using metaphor shows that metaphor is omnipresent.

It is so omnipresent that it informs our world views. As Lakoff and Johnson hold, metaphor is fundamentally conceptual in nature. By this they mean that human beings cannot conceive, think or act without metaphor (Lakoff and Johnson, 2003, pp. 3–6, 272). I take this to mean that metaphor "in-forms" human language, thought and action. To say that it "in-forms" human language and thought is to point out yet another metaphor, one especially important for this book. What is it to "in-form"? To "in-form" is to provide substance to the structure: to move into, inside of the form of the thing itself.

This is why the old adage "Sticks and stones may break my bones but names will never hurt me" is not true. Words do hurt because they inform our world views, the way we see others, the way we see ourselves. While the word *bastard*, for instance, has lost its original meaning, that meaning was devastating. The word once named children who had no publicly acknowledged father, no father who acknowledged paternity. To call someone a "bastard" was to insult him or her because he or she lacked a father. To lack a father was to be in jeopardy. It meant that one had no paternal family name, no chance to inherit, no place in the patriarchal social order. Bastards were disruptive because they were a manifestation of a broken society. They had no father to guide them, no father to discipline them, and thus no father to initiate them into the larger community and its tradition.

The problem of bastardy is central to *Go Tell It on the Mountain*, James Baldwin's classic novel of difficult and degraded Harlem life after the Harlem Renaissance of the

1920s. John, the son at the centre of the novel, is illegiti-mate, a bastard. His mother has married another man, Ga-briel, who has taken this boy on as his stepson. However, as I will discuss in more detail in later chapters, this fa-ther-stepson relationship is fraught with problems. Gabriel looks at the boy and sees nothing but evil, nothing but a fundamental disruption of holiness. Why? Because the boy is a bastard, born of an illegitimate and illicit relationship. He has no name, other than what the stepfather grudgingly gives him, laced with sarcasm and verbal, sometimes even physical, abuse. Behind this mistreatment of John, as the novel reveals, lies Gabriel's failure to act as a responsible father to his first son, Royal, born of a torrid affair when Ga-briel was much younger. Gabriel abandons his own bastard child, who grows up to be a troubled man. Gabriel assumes fatherly responsibility for another's bastard, but is unable to love him.

To be sure, the problem of the bastard also points to the problem of the mother. At a time when women and thus mothers could not hold property, could not vote, and had no identity save that given to them by their fathers or husbands, bastards were bastards not because they didn't have a mother but because they didn't have a father. The mother was identifiable, the father not. The problem was that the mother could give nothing to the child, as far as the social order was concerned. In *Go Tell It on the Mountain*, the mother loves John, despite what her husband thinks or wants. But Gabriel abuses her as well as his stepson: the mother is also negatively marked by her bastard son. Gabri-el can't help but look at her and think that she is a tainted, weak woman.

We have come a long way from this world, thank goodness. Children, at least in North America, are no longer cursed by others in their communities because they lack fathers who acknowledge their paternity. This has been a liberating development for mothers and children. It speaks of a world in which mothers can provide legitimacy: as women, they now have the legal right to inherit and own property and to vote. It speaks of a world in which a child's identity is not uniquely and singly bound up in the father's name. In the West, at least, there is a growing emphasis on judging the child not on what the father's name says about him, but on what the child is and might become.

Albus Dumbledore, the headmaster of Hogwarts School of Witchcraft and Wizardry in J.K. Rowling's wildly successful Harry Potter novels, speaks to this phenomenon. As a champion of wizards and witches who are not "purebloods" (who come from non-magical parents and families), Dumbledore is fond of saying that many in the magical community too quickly value people not because of who they are or might become, but because of the name given to them by their fathers' families.

At the centre of the novels are two characters. One is Lord Voldemort, the metaphorical embodiment of evil, Nietzsche's *ubermench*, who killed his own non-magical father because the father had rejected both him and his mother. The other character is Harry Potter, himself the metaphorical embodiment of the daring, the good, the just. Voldemort killed Harry's parents in an attempt to kill Harry himself. Harry, now an orphan, loves his parents, even in their absence. The battle between Harry and Voldemort is, in many ways, a battle between what they have inherited from their fathers. Voldemort inherited rejection. Harry, at least as he imagines it, inherited valour. In the fourth book in the series, *Harry Potter and the Goblet of Fire*, Voldemort again tries to kill Harry. As they duel, Voldemort pitilessly reminds Harry that just as he, Voldemort, killed Harry's father, he will also kill Harry. Harry imagines himself as his father, standing upright, dying a valiant death.

However, the mitigation of the taint of the bastard has created, in part, a problem: fathers in some cases aren't seen as necessary at all. Indeed, in some cases, fathers—at least in the most basic sense of the term—have become wholly unnecessary through the process of artificial insemination. Lesbian couples, for instance, can now purchase sperm from a sperm bank that houses the genetic material of anonymous male donors. Via artificial insemination, children are born to these couples. It seems that society, on the whole, doesn't care whether or not there are fathers to pass on their names, disciplines and traditions.[4] Indeed, it seems evident that in these cases, society doesn't care whether there are fathers at all, if by fathers we mean male parents who (choose your metaphor) care for, provide for, protect their children. It may be the case that one lesbian partner assumes the male role in a relationship (whatever that role might be), but there is no father in the family.

Artificial insemination can be, in and of itself, a good thing. Witness the famous case of Lance Armstrong, seven-time winner of the Tour de France. When he discovered that he had testicular cancer, he had sperm removed and frozen. He and his then-wife were able to have children through artificial insemination. Who but the most hard hearted could deny that this is a good use of reproductive technology? Who but the most ardent defender of so-called natural reproduction could deny that this is a positive use of medical science? However, as Daniel Callahan points out, artificial insemination does have a shadow side for those of us who are concerned about the state of fatherhood. He writes, "Perhaps it was the case that fatherhood had already sunk to such a low state, and male irresponsibility was already so accepted, that no one saw a problem. It is as if everyone agreed: 'Look, males have always been fathering children anonymously and irresponsibly; why not put this otherwise noxious trait to good use?'" (Callahan, 1996, p. 166). The point here isn't to debate the merits of artificial insemination, in the abstract or in theory. I believe that it is, on the whole, a good technology. However, when used to create a child who will have no father other than the one who provided the genetic material necessary for human reproduction, artificial insemination does, indeed, make the idea of fatherhood problematic. Men become sperm donors and nothing else. As Callahan suggests, perhaps this is the logical result of a culture that has long accepted that men often share their sperm without being willing to accept the role of father. I remember working in a neighbourhood in the south side of Chicago where it was well known that teenage males took pride in adding another child to the world without becoming its father in more than the biological, genetic sense.

In other cases, the father is necessary but uncelebrated, unwanted, unmentioned. In the mid-1990s in Richmond, Indiana, a small town near the Ohio border, the local newspaper, the *Palladium-Item*, celebrated the pregnancies of 18-year-old twins, both of whom were pregnant at the same time. They were not married, and the fathers weren't even mentioned in the newspaper article. Rather, the paper played the cute angle: isn't it cute that twins are having babies at the same time? No mention was made of the potential problems in store: they were young mothers-to-be, still teenagers, and they had no partners to father their children. In many ways, this approach to the story shows that North American society is more compassionate today; no longer does it brand its unmarried pregnant women with a scarlet letter. In some ways, though, this is a problem: where are the fathers?

The word *bastard* now is an insult applied to a person who is particularly annoying, malicious even. It has moved from one domain of language, as Lakoff and Johnson teach us, to another; hence, it is a metaphor. It no longer refers to a child whose paternity is not acknowledged. Now, to be a bastard is to act in such a way that one is out of bounds; one has broken a social code that helps the community stay together.

Words, and metaphors in particular, can hurt and help because they inform our world views. As I wrote in an earlier book, the meaning of the phrase *view the world*, however, is not as obvious as it might first appear.[5] The word *view* is not used literally. While a person's world view might include what that person has seen of the world with his or her eyes, *view* comprises more than that. Viewing involves the other senses: what that person has heard and hears, what that person has felt and feels, what that person has tasted and tastes, what that person has smelled and smells. That person's view also includes emotion, cognition, memory, dreams. *View* encompasses that person's sight as this sight arises from the whole of that person.

For example, one father might watch another father play with his children and be overcome with longing because he has been separated from his own children for a long time and misses them desperately. A mother might view yet another father playing with his children and be brought to tears because her own ex-husband, the father of her children, is a deadbeat dad: he left her and their children years ago, and maintains no physical, emotional or financial contact, despite his promises to the contrary. A man might cry with joy while watching a movie in which a father is portrayed as tender, caring and immediately present in his children's lives, remembering his own late father. He recognizes, perhaps without being able to name it, that this fictional movie father—that his own father—acted in ways to help secure liberation for all concerned: with, about, by and for the act of fathering.

Metaphors inform, shape, sustain and challenge the ways we view the world and our places in it. Any father or mother can easily confirm this statement by watching their children at play. My own son, for instance, with me as his willing accomplice, spent much of his young life studying and embodying metaphors. One of the earliest was the Jedi Knight, metaphor for all that is good, brave and true. As a four-year-old, he would wear my Aikido outfit, rolled up to account for our size difference, and go on daring Jedi adventures, light sabre in hand. Then it was a baseball player, another metaphor for all that is good, brave and true. As an eight-year-old, he would spend hours in our yard, with me as his opponent, imagining himself to be various players old and new: Christy Matthewson, Babe Ruth, Roberto Clemente and Manny Ramirez among them. Jedi Knights and baseball players are metaphors, without doubt. They stand in the North American cultural narrative as symbols for values and realities that aren't, not really. They have shaped my son, and countless other sons and daughters, in ways that I can only guess at. Of course, they have shaped me, too: why else would I imagine myself to be Satchel Paige when I pitched to my son?

To be sure, we might not even be aware of the ways metaphors shape and challenge our world view. Some metaphors work obliquely, under the radar or in the shadows. Metaphors for fatherhood are such, I maintain. There has been precious little general discussion about the metaphors for fatherhood that pervade the North American cultural narrative, precious little analysis of those metaphors that name and shape fatherhood. Before that analysis can begin, however, we need to acknowledge that fatherhood, at least as defined by the metaphors the North American cultural narrative offers, is in crisis.

2

Fatherhood in Crisis

The whiskey on your breath
Could make a small boy dizzy;
But I hung on like death:
Such waltzing was not easy.

Theodore Roethke, "My Papa's Waltz"

The crisis in fatherhood is, in part, a symptom of the general crisis of postmodernity in which we find ourselves. The crisis is also a symptom of a disease that has been centred in the Roman Catholic priesthood but, to be sure, is a problem for all fathers: symbolic (as in the case of Roman Catholic priests) or literal.

The metaphors that are at the core of this book—father as deadbeat, father as thundergod, father as architect, father as fool and father as Mr. Mom—are in contest with each other. This is because we live ever conscious of the fact that our histories are ambiguous and our languages are plural.[6] We see in history that even the grandest and most heroic metaphors are fraught with problems. For example, even as the United States and Canada have developed into extraordinarily free societies, they have done so on the literal and figurative backs of human beings—black Africans and Aboriginal peoples first among them. We see that our language is only one among many and that it, too, while an agent of freedom, has also been an agent of oppression. As philosopher Jean-François Lyotard has said, we live among the ruins of the "metanarrative" of singular, unquestionable stories that guide us surely and safely through the vagaries of a chaotic and often dangerous world. History is too ambiguous, language is too plural for metanarratives and their constitutive metaphors to stand unquestioned. In short, we live amidst the ruins of postmodernity.

Among these ruins we find fatherhood. While historians have demonstrated that *fatherhood* has always been a contested term and practice, postmodernity has brought fatherhood into further crisis, theoretically and practically. Thus, we have a number of metaphors for fathers available to us, none of which is foundational. Who should a father be? How should a father be? There is no easy answer to these questions because, as Jeff Hearn has written, "Social realities, such as fatherhood ... should not be seen *a priori* as solid, unified, or singular; more usually, they are multiple, dispersed and sites of contradictions" (Hearn, 2002, p. 245).

A host of writers and politicians from a range of disciplines and perspectives has acknowledged this position. For a philosophical ethicist such as Daniel Callahan, the problem emerges when one takes seriously the "nasty phenomenon of more and more single-parent families, mainly headed by females, and a growing number of absent and neglectful fathers" (Callahan, 1996, p. 161). Former US vice-president Al Gore has claimed that fatherhood is the key to civilization (Gavanas, 2002, pp. 231, 272 n. 13). Others, such as sociologist Michael Kimmel and philosopher Thomas W. Laqueur, have helpfully traced the confused and confusing history of fatherhood, as has sociologist Ralph LaRossa. As LaRossa argues, "Caring and loving men have been denied the value of knowing that there were others before them, others who shared their concept of what good fatherhood meant. Thus, when a father of the 1990s decides to take a pen in hand and write about what it means to have sole responsibility for his children while his wife is out of town, there is little sense from the author that this is really not new" (LaRossa, 1997, p. 4). LaRossa reminds us that the history of fatherhood is so confused and confusing that fathers have little sense that their practice as fathers has a history. If one presumes that fathers have always acted as distant thundergods, as architects, as fools, one needs to think again. A careful analysis indicates that the history of fatherhood is not a monolithic narrative: alternatives have existed and do exist.

Fatherhood is also in crisis because we have seen, in the midst of postmodernity, a particularly ghastly metaphor for father arise: father as pedophile. Symbolically, Roman Catholic pedophiliac priests have given to us a spectre that haunts all parents' dreams. If these priests are fathers—and by practice and definition they are religious fathers—then perhaps fatherhood is wholly bankrupt; perhaps the world would be better off without fathers. Of course, pedophilia is not limited to symbolic fathers: biological and adoptive fathers have been and are pedophiles.

Given the issue of pedophilia, perhaps this chapter—indeed, this book—should have begun with the following two images.

Images
1

They didn't know until years later. It had been a wonderful evening of celebration. Friends and family gathered to mark the marriage of a young couple. Among those gathered was an old friend of the bride and her husband, stepfather to the old friend's daughter. By all accounts he was a good man: a good husband, a good father, a good worker. After the wedding and the reception, the 20-somethings decided to continue to celebrate, shifting to a dance club. The bride's old friend was torn. She wanted to join the others at the club, but she also needed to get home to her young daughter: the babysitter could stay only for so long. Her husband, the loving stepfather, insisted that she go on: he would go home to relieve the babysitter of her duties, to care for his stepdaughter.

A few years later, the bride, now a wife and mother herself, answered the phone. A close friend was on the line.

"John was arrested."

"What! Why?"

"Child molestation."

It came to be known that the good husband, the good worker, the good stepfather had been sexually abusing his stepdaughter for years. The evening that he left the wedding early in order to care for her took on a new meaning.

Images
2

In March 1991 a New Orleans television station broadcast an exposé about a local priest, Dino Cinel, of the parish of Saint Rita's. The affair dated back to late 1988 when large numbers of pornographic videos had been found in his rectory, and because most of them concerned pedophile themes, their mere possession constituted a criminal offence. Cinel had also produced pornographic videos and photographs depicting sexual encounters between himself and several teenage boys, and the scandal was intensified because these had occurred in the parish rectory. (Jenkins, 1996, p. 45)

◎ ◎ ◎

While it is difficult to imagine how the pedophile could be a legitimate metaphor for all fathers, the incidence of pedophilia among biological and adoptive fathers as well as symbolic ones (such as Roman Catholic priests) is high enough and troubling enough to give one pause. If some or even many literal fathers can violate the bodies and souls of their children, what might this say about all fathers? If some or even many Roman Catholic priests can violate the bodies and souls of children entrusted to them by their parents, what does this say about the symbol of fatherhood?

Pedophilia is a strange word, highly ironic when examined from the comparative vantage points of its roots and its current usage. Its first root word, *ped,* or even *paedo,* emerged from the Greek *paid* and *pais*, meaning child or boy, most often the former. A host of words with neutral or positive meanings use this root, chief among them *pediatrician.* Certainly, we see pediatricians as caretakers of the health of children and esteem them for the service that they provide.

Philia comes from the Greek *philia*, meaning, in the broadest sense, friendship, fondness, affinity for. A host of words with neutral or even positive meanings use this root. *Philharmonic*, for instance, suggests a friendship, a fondness, an affinity for harmony.

When placed together, these roots have an ominous denotation and ominous connotations within the contemporary North American cultural narrative. *Pedophilia* means, literally, a friendship, a fondness, an affinity for children.

However, one cannot be described as a pedophile without being ostracized and, most likely, a target for police investigation. As we all know, the word *pedophilia* is not neutral; it suggests something much more evil, much more deranged than simply friendship, fondness or an affinity for children. It both denotes and connotes sexual desire for, and abuse of, children.

When a biological or adoptive father becomes a pedophile, he violates social taboos, a spouse's trust, a child's need for care. When a Catholic priest becomes a pedophile, he violates social taboos, parents' trust, his charges' need for care. Both types of pedophiles call into question the validity of fatherhood. It would be easy to dismiss this challenge to fatherhood if pedophilia on the part of literal and metaphoric fathers were anomalous, limited and relatively unique. However, it is not, as we now know.

The North American cultural narrative does not offer simply images of pedophilia; it also offers images of repressed pedophilia, as we see in the film *Mr. and Mrs. Bridge*, starring Paul Newman and his real-life wife, Joanne Woodward. Mr. and Mrs. Bridge, the title characters, live a comfortable and stilted suburban life in the late 1950s. He is an insurance man; she is a housewife. They are proper, controlled, relatively sexless and emotionless. For instance, Mr. Bridge's devoted secretary—single, alone and lonely—finally confesses what she has long kept to herself: she is in love with Mr. Bridge. When she invites him to her bed after he gives her a drive home, he rejects her offer and leaves her at her apartment. He does not, cannot, acknowledge her feelings. He simply denies her and drives away.

However, Mr. Bridge, we come to see, is not bloodless, not without sexual desire. In another scene he looks out the window of his bedroom. Sunning themselves in the family's backyard are his voluptuous daughter, who is in her late teens, and her equally shapely friend. They are on the verge of womanhood and the wildness of the 1960s. As he watches them, he sees the curves of their bodies, the rise and fall of their breasts as they breathe. He is aroused. Properly, but problematically nonetheless, he redirects his erotic desire. He finds his wife and surprises her. She submits and he is able to consummate his longing: the desire aroused by the daughter and her friend finds its sublimated consummation in his wife's body.

Is Mr. Bridge a pedophile? No. Is he driven by pedophiliac desire? Yes. Apparently. Although his daughter and her friend are nearly adults, they are children nonetheless, still too young to be part of adult eros and the adult erotic economy. We have to acknowledge as we watch him that some fathers are trangressors. They violate taboos and violate the bodies of children. It would be very easy to reject Mr. Bridge if he were a pedophile. Instead, he sublimates and redirects the eros his daughter and her friend awaken in him, finding a suitable outlet for his sexual energy. Still, the root cause must be taken seriously and not forgotten.

Pedophilia is not, of course, a new development. However, the recent revelations about pedophile priests and pedophile fathers highlight the crisis in fatherhood. Have there been admirable priests, points of light in a dark world? Of course. Have there been priests who violated their call by violating young boys? Clearly. Have there been admirable biological and adoptive fathers, points of light in a dark world? Absolutely. Have there been fathers who have violated all taboos by violating their own children? Yes. How can the term *father* ever again be used without hesitation? Is fatherhood ambiguous? Without question.

One need not turn to the dark extreme, however, to discover the problem of meaning that confronts fatherhood. Fathers across North America struggle in pedestrian ways amid the postmodern ruins of fatherhood.

What can be done? One option, obviously, is to give up, to become nihilistic, to accept the ambiguity and plurality and submit to confusion and even despair. The other option is to offer a new story, a metaphor open to change as the world changes. This is not meant to be yet another metanarrative that attempts to mask its nature. It is not meant to be a piece of dogma, guiding human life from above. It is not meant to be taken as an ideal form, existing above and beyond human life even as it guides it. Rather, it is a metaphor, a figure that might guide us as we move among the ruins. The crisis of fatherhood presents an opportunity for us to rethink the meaning of father and the practice of fatherhood. It is an opportunity to find a new metaphor that is both emancipating and redeeming. Even as we recognize and name father as deadbeat, as thundergod, as architect and as fool—and discard these metaphors for what they are, inadequate guides for the liberation of fathers and all those affected by fathers—we can find a healthier metaphor emerging.

◎   ◎   ◎

Liberation

What is it that fathers should do as fathers? When a man becomes a father, his identity is inexorably transformed. He is no longer simply a son, worker, husband or partner. He is a father. He will become known to his children's friends and acquaintances as "Bobby's father," as "Li's father." I still remember when my own father, with affection, told me the following story. When I was 19, I coached a swim team in our small Colorado town. When the mother of one of my swimmers met my father, a town businessman, she said, "You must be Brad's father." My own father had lost his individual name in the eyes of this mother. She could easily have said, "You must be Mr. Stull." After all, she knew my family name. Instead, she identified my father through me. For her, my father was known first and foremost by his relationship to her son's coach. So, too, in my turn have I become known by my relationship to my own children.

This discussion is important because it begins to open up a dense tangle: What is the purpose of the father as father? What should the father do? Who is the father? His role is to work for the liberation of his children and, by extension, himself and his children's mother. Why? And what is liberation? Both questions are deceptively easy to answer. Why should the father work for the liberation of his children? Because humans are meant to be liberated. What is liberation? It involves both redemption and emancipation.

This book's definition of *liberation* is taken from Schubert M. Ogden's book on liberation theology, *Faith and Freedom: Toward a Theology of Liberation* (Ogden, 1979).

This book is Ogden's rejoinder to liberation theology as it developed in Latin America. Thus, my discussion of liberation is marked by two caveats. First, I am borrowing from a work of theology, although I am not a theologian and this book is not a theological treatise. Second, Ogden ultimately grounds liberation in the activity of God. I don't disagree with Ogden, but I am concerned with much more earthly matters: how can fathers be agents of liberation in the lives of their children? The analogical connection is obvious, if not mundane. For Ogden, God acts as liberator in the lives of God's creation. For me, fathers should act as agents of liberation in the lives of their children. Thus, God is to father as creation is to child. This analogy shouldn't be taken too far, however, for three reasons.

First, mothers need to be included in this scheme. While this book is not about motherhood, I would argue that mothers, like fathers, are and should be agents of liberation in the lives of their children. Second, Ogden is speaking as a Christian theologian. My vision of fatherhood, rooted in the idea of liberating activity, applies not only to Christians but also to people of all faiths and none. Third, part of the liberation about which Ogden writes is far beyond the ability of mortal fathers. They cannot, however they might wish, save their children from death.

In short, Ogden argues that liberation involves "being liberated from bondage." Redemption, as an act of liberation, involves "liberation from the bondage of death, transience, and sin." Emancipation, as the other act of liberation, involves "liberation from all other forms of bondage, particularly the structural or systematic bondage ... that keeps us and our fellow creatures from realizing our fullest potentials" (Ogden, 1979, p. 99).

Importantly, the word *liberation* involves metaphor. If to liberate is to set free, or to release, we see at the metaphorical centre of the word something that *has been* captured and something that *has* captured. One cannot be set free unless one is held. One cannot be released unless one is contained.

This containment is bondage. At once metaphorical and literal, the word *bondage* speaks to being held captive by bonds, to being a slave, to being bound or tied up. The redemptive activity of liberation addresses the bonds and slavery of death, of transience, of sin. The emancipating activity of liberation addresses bonds and slavery of all sorts, among them metaphorical and literal prisons, metaphorical and literal torture, metaphorical and literal poverty.

Although, as I wrote above, mortal, earthly fathers cannot save their children from the inevitability of death, they can forestall the deaths of their children by providing the sustenance, housing and medicine necessary for their children to flourish. Some fathers ignore these necessities, hastening the end of their children's lives. Some even kill their children, surely acting counter to liberating activity in its most fundamental sense.

I would even suggest that most mortal, earthly fathers help their children not to sin. Why else do we teach our children some variant of the Golden Rule: do unto others as you would have them do unto you? While we may not want to call infractions of this rule "sins" in our modern, secular world, certainly these infractions are just that in the Greek sense of the word *sin*, which means "to miss the mark." At our best, we want our children to be at their best, to hit the mark.

When children do miss the mark, good fathers forgive them or help them find forgiveness. This forgiveness is not the divine forgiveness that Odgen envisions when he speaks of the redemptive power of God, but it is close, I suggest. When our children disrupt family harmony, as they all do, we forgive them as we teach them not to "miss the mark" in the future. Only dysfunctional fathers act otherwise.

At their worst, dysfunctional fathers themselves miss the mark in horribly profound ways, sexually, verbally or physically assaulting their children. Why we do not call such acts "sins" is an interesting question. We prefer to call them crimes, as if they were fundamentally offences against the legal order of the state. And they are. Calling them crimes allows us to prosecute the accused and try to make the situation right. However, such abuses are also offences against the humans that fathers are meant to care for. The abusive father is not only committing a crime. He is also committing an offence against the integrity of another human, subjecting this human to literal or metaphorical bondage, or both.

To be sure, children also act to redeem their fathers. When fathers are willing to listen to their children, to be open to them and their extraordinary lives, fathers can find redemption—at least the limited sort of redemption one human offers to another. I sometimes act as a thundergod with my own children, pontificating from on high, passing out terse and anger-filled directives in response to some mistake, usually minor, that they have made. As my son is moving into adolescence, he sometimes responds in kind. I see that I am teaching him to ape my thundergod tendencies: we turn into Zeus and his son, throwing lightning bolts at each other from our own mountains. Recognizing and understanding this one dimension of our relationship offers the opportunity of redemption. I don't want him to become a thundergod as a father, and I work to release the thundergod from myself. I ask, "Do I need to speak to him in this way?"

Fathers live not only in redemptive relationships with their children but also in potential and actual emancipating relationships with them. If bondage can be both psychic and physical, surely fathers—at least good, liberating, incarnate fathers—work to emancipate their children from such bonds. In turn, they can be emancipated themselves.

For instance, what father wouldn't work to release his child who has been imprisoned unjustly? While most fathers would learn to live, however uneasily, with the reality of a child justly imprisoned, no father, no liberating father, would learn to live with a child unjustly imprisoned. Why? Because the bonds of prison deny the child physical and psychic freedom to come to his or her full fruition.

Certainly, as Ogden says, one can find redemption even while in prison. This is why it is important to distinguish between these two dimensions of liberation. Malcolm X, as we see in his autobiography (Malcolm X, 1965), is a case in point. If any American was justly imprisoned, it was Malcolm X. It is true that he came from a family destroyed by racism. His father was killed by racist domestic terrorists; his mother was eventually hospitalized because of mental illness; his brothers and sisters separated each from the other. Malcolm was raised in racist America, an America that told him, brilliant student that he was, that African-Americans couldn't be lawyers. Still, Malcolm was responsible for the choices he made. He chose to become a thug, a criminal, a burglar, a numbers runner. Eventually, he wound up in jail.

While there, he found another father figure: Elijah Muhammad, founder and leader of the Nation of Islam, an African-American Muslim sect. Through Elijah's fatherly guidance, Malcolm X found redemption: he was able to find forgiveness for his sins and transgressions, for the degraded state into which he had devolved. This redemption did not bring about his emancipation. What it did bring about was a change so profound that when Malcolm X was released from prison, he rose to become the most eloquent and powerful leader in the Nation of Islam. He became the counterpoint to the work of Martin Luther King.

Elijah Muhammad and the Nation of Islam offered more than redemption to Malcom X. They offered him the physical and psychic tools he needed to make his emancipated state fruitful. They provided a job, a community of believers, a home. Elijah Muhammad took his fatherly role seriously: he worked for both redemption and emancipation.[7]

As Malcolm writes, however, his bondage began long before he went to prison. Even though he was physically free as a youth and teenager, he became increasingly bound by racism: his psyche was imprisoned by it, leading him to make choices that resulted in his eventual physical imprisonment. The watershed moment, perhaps, involved his beloved junior high school teacher, Mr. Ostrowski, who was, not insignificantly, a white man. During a conversation about careers, Mr. Ostrowski asked Malcolm what he wanted to be when he became an adult. Malcolm answered, "A lawyer." Mr. Ostrowski told Malcolm that he needed to choose a more realistic goal: perhaps a carpenter? a porter? African-Americans don't become lawyers, Mr. Ostrowski told Malcolm—despite the fact that Malcolm had performed brilliantly as a student. Malcolm was crushed and became debilitated by this bond placed on him. With neither a father nor a strong mother to help counter the psychic bondage of racism, he began his long journey from psychic to physical imprisonment.

Humans, including our children, are beset by psychic and physical forms of bondage from which they need to be emancipated. Is consumerism a form of bondage? Definitely. Sexism? Of course. Poverty? Without a doubt. Redemption is not enough, as Ogden realizes. If humans are to live to their full potentials, they need liberation: redemption and emancipation.

If a father has moved beyond a world view in which women are seen as second-class citizens, how can such a father not be concerned about the forms of bondage that continue to threaten his daughter? Men still sexually assault girls and women. Society still asks women to fulfill subservient roles in the social order. Girls, as a population, appear to lose their spark for science and mathematics when they become adolescents, despite the fact that they test higher than boys while in elementary school. Of course, these forms of bondage are particular to the North American context. In other parts of the world, girls are still sold into prostitution and worse. If a father doesn't want these fates to bind his daughter, then he himself is bound to work for emancipation, to teach his daughter how to find fruition in a world that would seek to entrap her.

As fathers work for the emancipation of their children, they themselves can become emancipated, freed from the psychic and physical bonds that might entrap them in certain world views, in certain ways of being in the world. Unfortunately, this was not a message that Elijah Muhammad wanted to hear from Malcolm X. Malcolm, late in his career with the Nation of Islam, came to hear rumours that Elijah Muhammad had had affairs and sired children out of wedlock, despite preaching against this type of activity. Malcolm confronted Elijah, who denied the rumours and rejected Malcolm's attempt to free his father figure—his metaphorical father—from the entrapment of lies and illicit behaviour. As a result, Malcolm ended his association with the Nation of Islam and converted to orthodox Islam, following a hajj to Mecca. Malcolm again lost a father, and soon was to lose his life, killed by assassins.

Other fathers have learned from their children, and have been set free as they work to set their children free. One such metaphorical father, as I will discuss in greater detail in chapter 5, is Mr. Kramer in the 1979 film *Kramer vs. Kramer*, which won an Academy Award for Best Picture in 1980. At first a distant father who builds his family only to stand back from it, Kramer has to confront fatherhood when his wife leaves him and their son in order to set herself free from the entrapment of a domestic scene that stifles her. By the end of the film, Mr. Kramer finds freedom in caring for his son, and comes to love his son in profoundly mundane ways: cooking for him, playing with him, talking to him, walking with him. Mr. Kramer is set free from the bondage of a particular way of being a father, a bondage that imprisoned him, his wife and their son.

Real, literal fathers have also found emancipation in relationship with their children, have been set free to become more fully human in their roles as fathers. Consider, for instance, the father who retires early to care for his school-age children—numbers five and six of six children—while his wife maintains an exceedingly busy practice as a physical therapist. Certain financial realities helped him: his wife makes a good living in her job; his father died, leaving him with some money. Still, he and his wife decided he would retire to become a stay-at-home dad, and his eyes light up when he speaks about being able to be there with and for his children.

If we can agree about what liberation is, we still need to explore why fathers need to work for the liberation of their children. On one hand, the answer to this might seem obvious. Why wouldn't a father want his children to be free? On the other hand, the answer isn't obvious, because many fathers do not want this, apparently. The deadbeat, the thundergod, the architect, the fool and even, to a lesser extent, Mr. Mom do not work for the freedom of their children, as chapters 2 to 5 will show. They themselves are not free, and thus they do not work as liberating agents in the lives of their children.

This book frankly presumes that freedom is the destiny of human beings, that freedom is fundamental and integral to the human project. The great leading lights of the 20th century point to this truth: Mahatma Gandhi, Martin Luther King, Dorothy Day, Oscar Romero, Cesar Chavez, Nelson Mandela, Archbishop Desmond Tutu, Pope John XXIII, Pope John Paul II, to name a few. If, indeed, freedom is our destiny, then fathers are integral to the movement of freedom: they can help to liberate their own children and thus themselves.

Martin Luther King claimed that the civil rights movement wasn't simply and merely about the liberation of African-Americans. It was that, to be sure; they had been psychically and physically bound since the time of slavery to a system that did not engender their freedom. However, as King sagely pointed out, the oppressors were in need of liberation as well. White Americans had come to see themselves as the prison keepers, thereby denying themselves the opportunity to be free, to find fruition. They were bound to an oppressor-oppressed relationship, thereby denying both themselves and African-Americans what Paolo Freire, another great champion of freedom, in his book *Pedagogy of the Oppressed* calls *subjecthood*.

By subjecthood, Freire means this: each person is free to become the subject of his or her history, rather then merely the object of someone else's.[8] Too often people work for each other's subjugation, even if unknowingly, unconsciously, unwittingly, instead of working for each other's liberation. Dictators are an obvious example of people who seek to objectify other humans, denying them the opportunity to be subjects in their own right. Fathers, however, can easily do the same. When a father, for instance, pushes his child to become something—a baseball player, a dancer or a doctor, for example—the father needs to be careful. Is this what the child wants? Is this choice going to help the child to be free, to find fruition? Or is this what the father wants? Is this choice going to help the father find fruition at the expense of the child? These questions are not easily answered. They can only be answered, finally, by unique and individual fathers living in unique and individual situations. Still, if freedom is human destiny, then fathers as fathers should work for their children's freedom, for their children's liberation from all forms of bondage, even those that fathers themselves place on children, even with the best of intentions.

How can fathers learn to work for liberation? One way, this book suggests, is to learn from the metaphors offered by the North American cultural narrative. These metaphors name and shape us whether we are aware of it or not. These metaphors can teach us the implicit and inherent wisdom of the culture as it moves toward greater and greater liberation. For fathers, I argue in this book, this liberation is to be found in incarnation. Not the incarnation of Jesus, although that certainly is the focus of liberation for Christians. Rather, fathers can find liberation and liberating activity in themselves as incarnate dads, willingly moving into the profoundly material world of their children's lives and acting as agents of freedom for themselves, their children and their partners. Before we turn to a full discussion of dad incarnate, however, we need to listen to and learn from the other metaphors offered by the North American cultural narrative, painful as they are.

3

The Deadbeat

"*Eli, Eli, lama sabach-thani?*"
[My God, my God, why have you forsaken me?]

—Jesus of Nazareth, on the cross

◎   ◎   ◎

Image

Sam had tired of his life, so he left. He left his wife and children for another woman, another child, another life. His first set of children became an asterisk to his life, a footnote. If one wanted to read his story deeply enough, one could find them. Every so often he would call, send a present, write. Even less frequently, he would send the child support money he had agreed to as part of the divorce settlement. If one wanted to read, not deeply at all, the stories of his first set of children, one could find him. His was the empty chair at the birthday party, the empty chair at Christmas, the empty chair at dinner every *night. Unfortunately, he wasn't Elijah, the risen prophet, for whom the family was waiting. He was the father, absent, and busy with another woman, another child, another life.*

© © ©

Jesus Abandoned and Abused

The word *deadbeat* usually connotes someone who has failed to meet his or her financial obligations. A deadbeat dad is a father who is behind on child support payments, which the court obliges him to pay. But *deadbeat* has another connotation, which involves psychic abandonment. Many deadbeat dads have abandoned their children not only financially, but also psychically. I suggest that financial abandonment is predicated on psychic abandonment.

Sadly, it is true that fathers who abandon and thus abuse their children are not only metaphorical: they exist in the flesh, and abandon the flesh of their flesh and thus abuse the flesh of their flesh. That said, they also exist in the realm of metaphor: our cultural narrative about fathers is informed by metaphors of abandonment and thus abuse. Just as real fathers abandon their children, metaphoric fathers do likewise. The North American cultural narrative imagines and reimagines these fathers, telling their stories and the stories of their children. Why? For many reasons: we all like tragedy; we all like to look at the pain of others, thankful that it is not our own; we all need to learn a lesson.

Few metaphors emerge out of nothing. The metaphor of the father who abandons, and again thus abuses, is no different. Our own 21st-century versions of such fathers have ancient antecedents, perhaps none more powerful than that of Jesus on the cross. If Jesus is the redeemer of the broken, then he is perhaps first and foremost the redeemer of the broken children who have been abandoned and thus abused by their own fathers. To be sure, this is a problematic claim, given the testimony about Jesus' father: he is not the God of abandonment and thus abuse, but, rather, the God of love.

Jesus himself, of course, was not a father, unproven tales of a secret marriage to and impregnation of Mary Magdalene aside. Jesus' involvement with fatherhood is what he reveals about his own father—that is, God, not Joseph—and what his story begins to tell us about fatherhood. Within the gospel narratives we see God, Jesus' father, only through Jesus' stories and, tragically, horribly, painfully, through the end of his life on the cross. The God who walked through the Garden of Eden looking for Adam and Eve, the God who presented himself as a burning bush to Moses, the God who appeared as a whirlwind to the attacking Egyptians is absent in the New Testament. The Lord of the Hebrew Bible no longer walks the earth, no longer visits his prophets and people. We have, instead, God present only through Jesus' testimony about his father: Jesus' words and life story trace the father who is absent.

On one hand, Jesus presents his father as the God of love, as the God who loves his creation.

"What is God like?" Jesus was asked over and over.

"What is the kingdom of God like?" Jesus was asked over and over.

Consistently, Jesus replied that God is the God of love and justice, that God's kingdom is the kingdom of love and justice. For example, this is precisely the point of the parable of the lost sheep in Matthew 18:12-14. Jesus draws an analogy between God and a shepherd, between God's people and the shepherd's sheep. The shepherd, Jesus tells us, cares for each of his sheep. He cares so much that when one is lost, the shepherd will search for and find it, even when he has 99 others that are safe. Had he been the manager of a modern industrial company driven by cost-benefit analysis, the outcome might be different. After all, he might ask, is it worth his time and energy to look for one sheep, a mere one per cent of his flock? Cost-benefit analysis might say no, it's not worth his time or energy. He could take the one per cent loss, move on and attend to the 99 sheep that remain. However, the shepherd is not driven by cost-benefit analysis. He is driven by love. He looks for, finds and reclaims the lost sheep. So, too, Jesus tells his listeners, does God. God might have hundreds, thousands, millions of people, but God cares for each individually. God would look for, find and reclaim the one.

Priests and ministers, who have for 2,000 years attempted to explain who Jesus was and why he has not yet returned (as had been and is expected), further Jesus' essential message about the love of God the father. When ministers and priests intone the famous phrase "For God so loved the world that he gave his only begotten son," they speak of a father God who, out of deep love, was willing to sacrifice his own child in order to save the created order. One can begin to understand the power of this extraordinary claim by imagining an earthly, mortal father doing the same.

If an earthly, mortal father could save the eternal souls of a large group of his neighbours only by turning his son over to state-sponsored torturers and executioners— knowing he would have to watch his son be tortured and die— would he accept?

It is hard to imagine that he would. We expect fathers to be heroic, to be willing to sacrifice themselves in place of their children. The father of a good friend of mine speaks to this expectation. Asked what fatherhood meant to him, this Methodist minister replied, "To kill or be killed for my children." We do not expect fathers, good fathers, to send their children to be tortured and killed, no matter what the cause. Fathers are expected to kill the torturers or even to take the place of their children, to be tortured in their stead.

Thus, in the J.K. Rowling's Harry Potter series, readers are reminded over and over again that the villainous Lord Voldemort killed Harry's father and mother as they tried to protect Harry from Voldemort's killing spell. Even as Harry himself faces Voldemort in *Harry Potter and the Goblet of Fire*, he thinks of his father. Near the end of the book, Voldemort has captured Harry and allows Harry the opportunity to duel with him. Harry's first reaction, in order to escape Voldemort's torturous spell, is to dive and hide behind a tombstone. Voldemort challenges Harry to come out. Harry decides not to hide like a child, not to die like a coward (for he is sure that he will die), but to die upright and proud, as his father did. Harry knew his father for only one year, yet the sacrifice that his father made impressed Harry so much that he wants to act like his father.

So too Darth Vader, the evil Sith lord in the epic Star Wars films, in his turn fulfills the terms of fatherly duty that we expect. In *Return of the Jedi*, the final installment of what is now a six-film series, Darth Vader sacrifices himself to save his son, Luke. He has to choose between good and evil, between the Jedi and the Sith, between himself and his son. After Luke defeats Vader in a light-sabre battle, the Emperor, Vader's Sith master, urges Luke to give in to his anger and kill his father. Luke, sensing that he is about to become evil, ignores the Emperor, throws his light sabre to the ground and lets his father live. The Emperor then turns on Luke, using his massive power to electrocute the young Jedi. As he writhes in pain on the ground, Luke calls to his father for help. Vader has to choose. He can let the Emperor kill his son, a fitting choice for the embodiment of evil, or he can intervene. He chooses the latter option, killing the Emperor to save his son, but the cost is great: he loses his own life. Before he dies, he asks Luke to remove the helmet that hides his grotesquely deformed face so that he might see Luke unimpeded. Luke removes the helmet and they are able to see each other face to face for the first time. Of course, Vader is no longer Vader at this point but Anakin Skywalker, Jedi knight. The father has emancipated his son from the killing power of the Emperor; the son has redeemed his father from the dark side of the Force, that ephemeral energy that pervades all existence.

In *Night*, Elie Wiesel's novel about the Holocaust, fathers do all they can to save, comfort and care for their sons in the midst of Nazi death camps. These fathers give their sons their last pieces of bread. They give their sons psychic comfort in the hell that was the camps. They give their sons succour even as the Nazis try to take it away.

These metaphorical fathers are what we uphold as the paradigm of good fathering. These fathers sacrifice themselves for their children, doing what is necessary to save them from harm.

So, what does it mean for us that in his ministry Jesus presents his father as the God of extraordinary love who, like the shepherd, cares deeply for each individual and, later, from his vantage point on the cross, feels abandoned by that loving God? Harry Potter, although sad that his own father is dead, never doubts that he was cared for. He knows that his father gave up his own life in order to save his son. Luke Skywalker sees with his own eyes his father's redemption from the dark side of the Force, sees with his own eyes his father's sacrifice on his behalf. Wiesel castigates himself at the end of *Night* for abandoning his father, given all that his father had done for him, given the fact that the father never once abandoned him.

Jesus, at least when he is near death on the cross, does not share Harry's, Luke's or even Wiesel's sense of connection to his father. The epigraph that opens this chapter is Jesus' plaintive cry from the cross, drawn from Matthew's Gospel. It is a paradigmatic moment of fatherly abandonment, at least from the momentary perspective of the suffering son.

The phrase that Jesus uses is drawn from Psalm 22, which, as John P. Meier holds, "is typical of those psalms of lament in the OT which begin on a note of desperation and end on a note of joy and thanksgiving" (Meier, 1980, p. 349). Seen within its larger textual context, Jesus' cry cannot be seen as the final word. It is the case, as Meier holds, that the gospel story ends with affirmation: Jesus, after all, rises from the dead on Easter morning: the father has not forgotten him, which indeed is the hope of Psalm 22 and the conclusion of the Gospel.

Yet, as Father Daniel J. Harrington, S.J., maintains about Jesus' use of the psalm, "the words of the psalm express most appropriately his feelings of abandonment and his subsequent reaffirmation of his total trust in the Father" (Harrington, 1983, p. 110). Note Harrington's use of the word "abandonment." For this moment in the gospel narrative, Jesus does indeed feel abandoned, whatever the larger context of the psalm suggests. Even Meier, who cautions us not to "indulge in the pulpit rhetoric or contemporary existentialistic interpretation which sees Jesus as falling into momentary atheism," also cautions us not to think that Jesus is "disinterestedly saying the breviary on the cross. His pain and anguish are real" (Meier, 1980, p. 349).

So, how do we interpret this moment? Do we simply set Jesus' cry within the larger context of both the psalm and the Gospel, and gloss over Jesus' feeling that he has been forsaken?

One might be quick to invoke Shakespeare and claim that "all's well that ends well." After all, according to the Gospels, to St. Paul, to the witness of Christians worldwide,

Jesus was not abandoned, did not die an eternal, godforsaken death. However he might have felt at the most painful and lonely moment of his torturous demise on the cross, he would soon be raised from the dead, brought to the metaphorical right hand of the father. However powerful and true this claim of faith might be, this exclamation of the power of God's love to defeat even death, we must take seriously Jesus' feelings on the cross as they are presented in the story. Jesus felt God-forsaken, God-abandoned, God-deserted. He felt, in his ultimate moment of need, that his father God had delivered him unto torturers and executioners as if to say, "Do unto my son as you will." They did so, whipping, mocking and crucifying him.

Christian theologians would argue that such was the divine plan. God rendered Jesus, his son, unto the torturers and executioners as the final paschal sacrifice. Jesus, as the Lamb of God, was not simply tortured and executed; he was sacrificed to break the hold of death. For whatever mysterious reason, God needed to have his own son killed so that death might be beaten. But one must still ask: How could a loving father willingly send his own son off to be tortured and killed, standing back, waiting for the cosmos to be righted?

Trinitarian theologians claim that Jesus is co-eternal with God the father. I suggest that Trinitarian theology arose in part because early Christian theologians, at least implicitly, asked: If Jesus is abandoned by God to suffer on the cross, how does this abandonment manifest divine love? The answer is this: If Jesus the Son suffers, God the father suffers. If Jesus the Son is abused, God the father is abused. If Jesus the Son is abandoned, then God the father is abandoned. God did not just send his son off to die. Insofar as God the father and God the son are part of the same godhead, God the father suffers, is abused, is abandoned.

This theological interpretation is interesting, exciting, important. But I suggest that it fails because it doesn't take the gospel story as seriously as it might. Jesus, at least as the Synoptic Gospels (Matthew, Mark and Luke) present him on the cross, feels separated from his father. He feels that his father is not with him. He feels that his father has left him to die an ignominious death.

Some might claim that Jesus knew he would be raised on the first Easter: he was, after all, co-eternal with the Father. Thus, his feeling of abandonment, his feeling that he was given up by the Father to be abused and killed, was tempered by the knowledge, or at least the hope, that he would rise again. This is the interpretation C. S. Lewis offers in *The Lion, the Witch, and the Wardrobe*, the most famous of the seven books comprising the Chronicles of Narnia. Aslan the lion is a metaphor for Jesus. The White Witch, queen of winter, who holds all of Narnia under her dictatorial regime, is evil incarnate. The wardrobe is the passageway between earth and the extraordinary world of Narnia, sung into creation by Aslan himself, with the approval of the Emperor over the Sea, who is a metaphor for God the father. Through this wardrobe, four children enter Narnia—two "sons of Adam" and two "daughters of Eve": Peter, Susan, Edmund and Lucy.

The White Witch knows that her reign of terror is threatened: old prophecies claim that when two sons of Adam and two daughters of Eve come to Narnia, they will defeat her and thus return Narnia to its rightful rulers: Aslan and the Emperor over the Sea. The White Witch soon lures Edmund to her side so that he will give his siblings up to her.

When Aslan, who has returned to Narnia, learns of Edmund's treachery, he offers to fulfill the terms of the Emperor's "deep magic." Although any traitor belongs to her and his blood must be spilled, Aslan offers to be executed in Edmund's stead. The White Witch cannot resist. The night of the execution, Aslan is fearful but determined. Susan and Lucy watch the horror unfold from a hidden spot. After Aslan is killed, they are bereft.

They wake the next morning to find that Aslan is gone. Then they hear him: Aslan in his full strength is alive, raised from death. Aslan and the girls romp in a flowering meadow, rejoicing over the miracle of his resurrection. He reveals to them that there exists an even deeper magic, which says that if a pure, innocent, sinless being is executed in place of the traitor, then all will be set right: the traitor's actions will be forgiven and the sinless being will rise to live again.

If we assume that Lewis' narrative can be interpreted as Christian allegory, we can begin to understand anew the profundity of Jesus' story relative to his feeling of abandonment. Aslan reveals that he had knowledge of a deeper magic. The Emperor over the Sea had wisely foreseen the possibility of what happened and accounted for it in such a way that the White Witch herself did not know of it: Evil did not know of what Good intended. It is true that Aslan was not certain that the deeper magic would work, but he did know of it and this knowledge informed his strategy.

He did not lie on the executioner's table and cry out to the Emperor over the Sea, wondering why he had been abandoned to the enemy. Aslan courageously chose to sacrifice himself with the hope, born of the knowledge given to him by the Emperor over the Sea, that this sacrifice, horrible and painful as it was, was not sacrifice of the self at all, but rather a transformation. Aslan moved from one self to another, and in fact his second self was material: he remained in Narnia, a flesh-and-blood lion capable of leading his followers against evil. Jesus, in contrast, felt abandoned by his father, God. No secret knowledge had been given to him to temper his death, to inform whatever strategy Jesus might have had. Further, Jesus never returned in material, earthly form. He became a new self, a self that was taken up into heaven, with the promise of coming again. Of course, this promise has not yet been fulfilled, and this is the reason for the history of Christianity: the Church has spent 2,000 years attempting to deal with the fact that Jesus died and left. Theologically, the Church claims, in Trinitarian fashion, that the Holy Spirit is now present instead of Jesus. Just as the Father gave the Son, so the Son sent the Spirit to sustain God's children. However, the Spirit is decidedly lacking, according to the children: they still long for the Son, for the Father. Just as the Lord no longer walked the Earth in the time of Jesus, the Lord has not walked the earth since Jesus' time. The New Testament only presents the Father through the testimony and life of Jesus. Since those times, the Father is only apparently present in the movement of the Spirit. Granted, Trinitarians claim that this is the presence of God. Still, it seems a rather absent presence. First, the Lord walks among us. Then, for Christians, the Lord sends his son.

When the son is gone, a material-less spirit is present. God, the father, is now three-times removed.

Attempts to justify the apparent feelings of abandonment that Jesus felt are understandable but problematic from the point of view of readers who take narratives seriously. These attempts turn the Gospels, as they report the death of Jesus on the cross, into farce: Jesus cries not out of pain and loneliness, but out of fiction. These interpretations would have us believe that Jesus knows that all would be right in the end. However, if this is so, then the cross is meaningless for all who would follow Jesus. He does suffer like we do. As the narrative presents it, Jesus does indeed suffer, does indeed feel abandoned. The God who calls him to set into motion a revolutionary movement leaves him to die, alone, on Golgotha, the hill of skulls: only the faithful women are with him. His Father, to whom Jesus points as a paradigm of love and justice, gives Jesus up to die, not a quick and merciful death but a death caused by asphyxiation.

One could say that, within the terms of the gospel stories as they describe Jesus dying on the cross, God the father seems to be a deadbeat. God has apparently abandoned Jesus psychically. The Christian narrative would have us place this apparent abandonment and abuse within the larger context of the Easter story: Jesus' subsequent resurrection is the ultimate sign of God's redeeming love and fatherhood at its best.

Thus, one could argue that the story of Jesus is divine irony: God takes on human form and dies a human death in order to redeem a fallen people. But as the Nobel prize–winning author Jose Saramago, in his novel *The Gospel*

According to Jesus Christ, points out, the price of redemption is blood and suffering, not only of Jesus but also of those who follow him, of those who have gotten in the way of those who follow him. Saramago reveals all this in a memorable sequence in which God the father, Jesus and Satan sit in a boat together in the middle of a lake and discuss what is to come (Saramago, 1994, pp. 305–333). God has ordained the death of his son because it will bring to fruition God's desire to become less of a regional God, to become a global God who commands the obedience and faith of millions and millions, many of whom would kill and be killed for God and his son. Jesus agrees to the plan because he has no choice: God the father is God the father, after all. However, as he dies on the cross, Jesus realizes that he has been tricked, that the world will be tricked: "Remembering the river of blood and suffering that would flow from his side and flood the globe, he called out to the open sky, where God could be seen smiling, Men forgive Him, for He knows not what He has done" (377). Jesus final words to the world in Saramago's novel are words of forgiveness. Yet, he does not call on God to forgive the world, as the gospels would have us think. Rather, Saramago inverts the call: Jesus calls on the world to forgive God. In his desire to become a global God, in his desire to satiate his need for sacrifice, God gives up his own son to a horrible death so that others will be inspired to worship Him and his son, even unto death. This Father God is not about the liberation of his children. Rather, he is about himself: he acts to create what he himself wants. People exist to serve him, to sacrifice and be sacrificed for him.

True, many Christians are paragons of love: Martin Luther King, Oscar Romero, Dorothy Day, Desmond Tutu, to name just four famous figures. In the cases of King and Romero, however, Saramago's novel names the issue: their greatness led to their own blood sacrifice. Assassins' bullets slaughtered both. At the same time, many Christians, in the name of a loving God, have slaughtered the innocent and guilty alike. Christian European culture, after all, gave birth to the Crusades. Christian German culture gave birth to Nazism and the Holocaust. Christian American culture gave birth to the Trail of Tears, the forced relocation of the Cherokee tribe in 1838. Why? All to propagate a vision of a social order based on an understanding of the God who sent his own son to the cross, who abandoned him on Golgotha. God the father is open to interpretation: presence is the partner of abandonment; self-sacrifice is the partner of the sacrifice of others.

Does the North American cultural narrative offer other contemporary metaphors of the deadbeat? Indeed, it does. These metaphors show us that the deadbeat is not dead in the North American consciousness and that the cultural narrative consciously attempts to name the deadbeat and expunge it. All these visions point to this obvious claim: the deadbeat metaphor is alive but would be better off dead. This is true both for the "public" and "private" spheres. *Public* refers to the civic nature of fatherhood. *Private* refers to the internal family dynamics.

The Public Deadbeat Dad

It must be said that current cultural practice in North America does little to approbate deadbeat dads, especially those who are psychically more than financially deadbeats. A poster of deadbeat dads hangs in the window of a liquor store in New Hampshire: it names fathers who are remiss in their child support payments and who have also left the scene of their crime. The state can't find them and so it appeals to the public for help. The narrative is clear. The bad guy has done a bad thing, and the public is called upon to defend the powerless: the village's children. One can't find a poster, however, of dads who are psychically deadbeat, who may pay their child support but who do not have a meaningful relationship with their children.

A father can abandon his children emotionally and society does not blink.

Often the deadbeat dad is part of the background, simply forgotten: the mother and the children are the ones who pay the price for the social outrage.

Consider, for instance, *The Scarlet Letter*, Nathaniel Hawthorne's famous novel about adultery and fornication among the Puritans. Though published in 1850, it is both foundational and current: it names our own reality, and demonstrates the way in which the narratives that inform our lives are often deeply rooted in our culture. The novel centres on Hester Prynne and her daughter. Hester wears the infamous scarlet *A*, a badge of approbation that marks her as an adulteress and fornicator. How does her community know that she had sex outside of marriage? She has a daughter. In general, women cannot hide their maternity. Men, on the other hand, can hide their paternity. The father does not bear the mark of the baby on and in and from his own body, for the world to see. Men can propagate with relative anonymity, relative immunity. Men can blame other men for the baby, even though DNA testing can refute their claims.

Thus, Arthur Dimmesdale—Hester's sexual partner and the father of their daughter—can hide himself in *The Scarlet Letter*. The fact that he is a clergyman allows Hawthorne to poke fun at a hypocritical personage in Puritan culture, suggesting that the very people who profess and defend the highest of family values are also the ones who debase and devalue them.

Although Dimmesdale is eventually held accountable for his actions, it is the mother and child who are outcasts. The father is deadbeat, but the mother and child pay the father's dues.

The resonant link between Hawthorne's tale of Puritan adultery and Saramago's treatment of God the father in *The Gospel According to Jesus Christ* can't be ignored. If Dimmesdale is a Puritan representative of God the father, then his actions, seen in the light of Saramago's narrative, are quite normal. If God the father abandons Jesus, then indeed the representatives of God the father can and do abandon their offspring as well.

Anyone who believes in God after the Holocaust must ask this question: If God the father loves his children, where was he when his chosen people, the children of the Abrahamic covenant, were being gassed in Auschwitz? This is the question at the centre of the work of Elie Wiesel and other Holocaust authors. In a justly famous scene in Wiesel's *Night*, God is put on trial. The rabbis ask, "Is God guilty of abandonment, of failing to fulfill the promises made to Adam, to Abraham, to Isaac, to Jacob, to Noah?" After all, if God was a just God who kept his promises and took seriously his commitment to his children, would he allow the Nazis to systematically exterminate Abraham's descendants? The rabbis conclude that God is guilty, that he has, indeed, abandoned his children. In other words, the rabbis conclude that God is a deadbeat.

Moreover, *Night* hints that God is such a deadbeat that he is, in fact, dead. At one point in the novel, a group of resisters is discovered in the camp in which Wiesel and his father are imprisoned. Among their members is a child. In order to scare the inmates and thus discourage resistance to the camp's regime, the child is hanged publicly for all the camp's inmates to see. A man in the crowd, viewing the dangling body of the child, asks, "Where is God now?" Another replies, "Here He is—He is hanging here on this gallows" (Wiesel, 1960, page 62).

At least two interpretations of this scene are possible. One is that Wiesel is borrowing from Christian ideology to make a claim about the suffering God. According to this interpretation, when God the father's people suffer, God the father likewise suffers. When God the father's people are killed, God the father likewise is killed. This is a vision of the empathetic God, the God who is able to enter into the suffering world of humanity and feel our pain. The problem with this interpretation is that *Night* offers no resurrection. God the father might die with us, but there appears to be no reward: the bodies do not rise again, or, if they do, only as skeletal ghosts. *Night* ends with a haunting image of Wiesel looking at himself in the mirror when the camps are liberated: he sees himself as a skeleton, bereft of his earthly father and his heavenly one.

The other interpretation of this scene is that God the father is indeed dead. The father God who claimed eternal devotion to the children of Abraham abandoned his children to the death camps and, as a result, is killed. This is not a vision of the redemptive father God biding his time until the right moment to enter into the lives of his suffering children at their hour of greatest need in order to save them. This is a vision of God the father who abandons and, in his act of abandonment, is killed. He is weak; the Nazis take advantage of that weakness and slaughter him as they slaughter his children.

In fact, *Night* can be read as an elegy for fatherhood. God the father is dead, but so are all fathers, even those earthly ones who are fathers working for the liberation of their children. The Nazis, *Night* reveals, destroyed not only God the father but all fathers: the family is defunct. As such, God has abandoned his role as liberating agent. No longer does he save his people from bondage in Egypt. Rather, he abandons them to Pharaoh and Pharaoh's wrath.

Consider, for instance, the end of Wiesel's novel. As a guard is beating Wiesel's father, he calls to his son for aid, water and comfort. Wiesel does not act: he fears for his own life and thus leaves his father to suffer and die alone. The empathetic reader might suggest that, since Elie Wiesel is only a boy, how can he do otherwise? What would be the point of his being beaten and killed, too? Wiesel, however, does not easily allow this empathetic response. He holds himself responsible for his failure to come to the aid of the father he dearly loved, who did all he could to help his son as they lived the horror of the camps.

This scene must be read in conjunction with other scenes throughout *Night* when sons abandoned their fathers. One, for instance, took bread from his own father, a father who gladly would have shared. Another left his own father to die alone on a forced march so that he himself could live. *Night* is a novel of the death of fatherhood: God the father is guilty and thus found hanging; earthly fathers who love their sons are abandoned by these very sons. The Nazis' greatest crime, perhaps, was the way in which they rent asunder familial ties and buried the fathers, divine and human.

But God and vicious enemies aren't always involved when the cultural narrative speaks about the deadbeat dad. Fathers themselves, the narrative tells us, are capable of acting as deadbeats, emotional or financial, without others' help. Consider the example in George Eliot's novel *Daniel Deronda*, published in 1876. Though written by a British author, it is nonetheless part of the North American cultural narrative. Like *The Scarlet Letter*, it sets the foundation. At one level the novel is a romance, involving Gwendolen Harleth, a beautiful and hedonistic narcissist; Daniel, a human manifestation of goodness and nobility; and Mirah, a young

Jewish singer. Daniel, who eventually learns that he is Jewish, is attracted to both women, but falls in love with Mirah. Gwendolen, meanwhile, marries well, but to a mean man who is the mirror of her own hedonistic and narcissistic self.

It is also a novel about fathers, and the theme of fatherhood is intimately linked to the rest of the narrative. *Daniel Deronda* presents the image of a deadbeat dad (Henleigh Mallinger Grandcourt) set against images of an emerging dad incarnate (Daniel's guardian, Sir Hugo) and a full-blown thundergod (Daniel's maternal grandfather).

Daniel calls Sir Hugo "uncle" or, more affectionately as Sir Hugo as taught him, "nunc." When Daniel once asked Sir Hugo about his parents, Sir Hugo replied that they had both died and that is why Daniel came to live with Sir Hugo. But the tales of the illegitimate sons of popes and cardinals, combined with his reading of Shakespeare and literature that dealt with unacknowledged sons, raised in Daniel's thirteen-year-old mind the possibility that Sir Hugo, "the uncle whom he loved very dearly," was his father (Eliot, 2003, p. 167). Indeed, many in society thought so, and Sir Hugo was aware of this (174). However, Sir Hugo didn't mind that people thought so. In fact, "he was pleased with that suspicion." Why? Because Sir Hugo was delighted with Daniel, "as fond of him as could be" (174). He raised him like a son, even though, as the reader suspects and comes to know, Daniel wasn't. Nonetheless, the love that Daniel and Sir Hugo feel for each other is that of father and son. Sir Hugo, as dad incarnate, works for Daniel's liberation, to give him freedom to become what he might become.

Sir Hugo's nephew and heir, Henleigh Mallinger Grand-court, who woos and marries Gwendolen, has fathered four children by a mistress, Mrs. Glasher, for whom he provides financially. Gwendolen knows about his children, but marries him anyway for his money and power.

She meets Mrs. Glasher and two of the four children. The matter of great import is this, in Mrs. Glasher's own words: "Mr. Grandcourt ought not to marry any one but me. I left my husband and child for him nine years ago. Those two children are his, and we have two others—girls—who are older. My husband is dead now, and Mr. Grandcourt ought to marry me. He ought to make that boy his heir" (152). She continues with this damning statement: "It is not fair that he should be happy and I miserable, and my boy thrust out of sight for another" (152). The boy is in the shadows, however: while he should be at the forefront of Grandcourt's thoughts, he is but a shimmering figure in dim light, trapped by circumstances he did not create.

Two monumental problems in Western thought and experience are at play in this scene. First is the place and role of women relative to men. Gwendolen sees in Mrs. Glasher all she dearly wishes to avoid: a life captured and held captive by a man.

More relevant to this study of fatherhood, however, is the second problem: the bastard child. Mrs. Glasher rightly fears that if Mr. Grandcourt were to marry Gwendolen and father a legal son with her, he would fully abandon his first son, who is illegitimate. As it stands, Mrs. Glasher has some hope that Mr. Grandcourt will come to acknowledge his son as his heir, but this hope rests on the first son not being supplanted by another.

It is clear that although Mr. Grandcourt supports Mrs. Glasher and their children financially, he is emotionally a deadbeat. He has no real connection to them. They exist on the periphery of his life, socially outcast.

◎　　◎　　◎

The Private Deadbeat Dad

By *private deadbeat*, I refer to the private effects of the father who abandons, as depicted in the North American cultural narrative. Rather than focusing on external, civic ramifications, this strand of the narrative traces for its readers internal family dynamics. It asks how families deal with the deadbeat and those the deadbeat leaves behind. In addition, it allows readers to understand the ironic place of the father who abandons: he might be seen as virtuous by the larger social order, but he is, in actuality, less than virtuous, even in his own eyes.

Gabriel is the deadbeat father of James Baldwin's novel *Go Tell It on the Mountain*. In Gabriel we see in one father a multiplicity of relationships with children, all of whom he fails. He abandons his first son; the abandoned son becomes a wild child and is, as an adult, stabbed to death in a fight. *Go Tell It on the Mountain*, read in relation to *Daniel Deronda*, helps us to remember that the deadbeat dad figures across time and space, race and class. Grandcourt belongs to the 19th century, Gabriel to the 20th. Grandcourt belongs to England, Gabriel to the United States. Grandcourt belongs to the landed gentry, Gabriel to the working class. Grandcourt belongs to the race of those who were once masters, Gabriel belongs to the race of those who were once slaves.

We learn from Florence, Gabriel's older sister, that Gabriel was himself the son of a deadbeat. Their father left the family soon after Gabriel was born (Baldwin, 1952, p. 72), never to be seen or heard from again. We also learn that Gabriel was a wild boy and as a young man, a drinker, carouser and womanizer.

After Gabriel finds Jesus, as related in his prayer (92–150), Gabriel becomes a renowned preacher and model of virtue. In his virtuous state, he receives a vision in which God promises him that his "seed" will carry the "seal" of the Lord (112). He even goes so far as to ask Deborah, who had been disgraced because she was raped as a teenager (73), to marry him (112–113). Gabriel chooses her to be his "holy helpmeet" (112), the woman who will enable him to make his vision become reality. Thus Gabriel sees himself as a new Abraham, the anointed father of anointed children.

But he and Deborah cannot have children; Gabriel commits adultery with a young woman named Esther and has a son, whom he names Royal, with her.

Gabriel, a man of God, commits a sin, violates the sexual taboos of the community and fathers a child out of wedlock. Like real men in real life, Gabriel rejects the child even before it is born.

Even when Esther dies, Gabriel never acknowledges that the son who grows up as a stranger to both father and God (138) is his.

Gabriel's rejection of his son doesn't mean that he forgets that his son exists. Rather, he watches Royal grow in wildness (139) and even prays that his son will not go to war during World War II (140–141). Gabriel is tormented by the presence of his son, by his wildness, and by the chance that he will die. Still, Gabriel will not acknowledge him.

The acknowledgment comes with his son's death in a knife fight.

News of Royal's death sends Gabriel into the depths of silent tears, crying for the loss of the son about whom he had dreamed, the son he rejected. Deborah then asks what she had known all along: "That Royal ... he were your flesh and blood, weren't he?" (147). Gabriel finally acknowledges to his wife what he had so long denied: Royal was indeed "my son" (148). Deborah then castigates Gabriel on two counts. First, because he treated Esther so badly, "sent her away" to "die, all by herself" (148). Second, and this is perhaps the most ironic part, because Deborah would have accepted Royal as her own child, would have raised him as her own son (149). Thus, Gabriel's status as a deadbeat father is forever sealed. He is revealed to be one who fully participated in Royal's violent demise. He was not a liberating agent in his son's life. Rather, in his pious cowardice, he abandoned his son to a life bounded by violence and death.

Gabriel has nothing to say to Deborah, except that he accepts her rebuke and knows that he must wait for redemption for what he has done (148). And yet, when Gabriel gets another chance to become a father, he fails. No longer is he a deadbeat, however. He accepts his role as father but responds to the children not with love, but with the belt; not with care, but with the fist. He becomes a thundergod, the deliverer of lightning, of fire, of unbending and unforgiving laws that, when breached, lead to punishment.

4

The Thundergod
and the Architect

"Lord of the manor"
"King of the castle"
"A man's home is his castle"

◎   ◎   ◎

Images

1

"Wait until your father gets home. Then you'll get it."
And indeed they did. Dan would arrive exhausted after a day's
work, but when their mother, his wife, told him how they had
not listened to her, how they had fought her and each other, how
they had made a mess of things, he laid down the law. A slap
or a spanking was not out of the question, but in the main he
used only his voice: raised powerfully, pointed directly at them,

he would threaten them, cajole them, verbally beat them until they agreed to behave.

◎   ◎   ◎

Images
2

Steven loved having his children at home. Even though they were now adults, establishing lives of their own, he wanted them to come home to the house in which they had been raised. He and their mother still lived there, although it was far too big for them alone. They kept it as a financial investment: they had paid off the mortgage and so owned it outright. Because the housing market was booming, its value increased tremendously each year. They also kept it as a nest for the children to return to, a place of gathering where all the disparate members of the family, now a widespread flock, could congregate for holidays, for birthdays, for simple days.

However, he didn't play with the kids or the grandkids. He never really had. He had been and was still a busy physician. He loved his children, but his contribution to their lives, he told himself when he bothered to think explicitly about it, was material and financial. He paid for the house, for their private school educations, for college. He even contributed to the purchase of their own homes: such was his duty and pleasure. But, when the children and grandchildren would congregate, he could be found, more often than not, in his basement workshop, content to hear the talk, the laughter, the tears, knowing that all was in good order.

◎   ◎   ◎

A Man and His Castle

As the last chapter argued, the North American cultural narrative about fathers is laced with deadbeats. They are real and imaginary, substantive and metaphorical. Thankfully, they aren't the only metaphors for fathers available. If they were, North American life would be more chaotic, more horrific, than it is. All children would suffer enormously and so would social order.

Father as thundergod and father as architect are important and powerful precisely because they have arisen from, are part of, and continue to support the religious, mythological and ideological foundations of North America. Father as thundergod and father as architect are also problematic because, as the North American cultural narrative reveals, they are not agents of liberation: they do not and probably cannot serve the long-term need for redemption and emancipation that is part of the lives of fathers and those involved with these fathers.

These metaphors are included together in the same chapter for three reasons. First, they live inversely to each other. Unlike the deadbeat, the thundergod and the architect are "involved" in their children's lives, albeit in very different ways. Each acknowledges the fact that they are fathers, that they have children. Second, each is linked "theomythically." By this I mean that each is a manifestation of understandings of god, albeit in opposition to each other. The thundergod is the pontificating lawgiver, like Zeus throwing thunderbolts from on high. The architect is the removed watchmaker of the cosmos: he makes it, he names it, he watches it tick from afar. Third, these theomythic manifestations can, interestingly, be found in metaphors of castle and kingship as they are used relative to fathers in the North American cultural narrative.

The epigraphs that open this chapter are emblematic of this link. Consider the last one: "A man's home is his castle." This commonplace phrase, often said jokingly, even sarcastically, initially links man to royalty. Obviously, *man*, here, is not open to a gender-neutral interpretation. This man is that gendered being who is different from woman; he has XY chromosomes, has the male sex organ, and acts in ways, however varied and constructed by the culture, that show his fellow humans that he is a man. Never, for instance, unless high irony were at play, would one see an advertisement in which an image of a woman is framed by this phrase, as if the phrase signifies her, or hear this phrase and picture a woman.

The explicit metaphor declares that this man's home is his "castle." Is it, literally? No, at least for most men, who live in modest homes. Even the wealthiest among us, those whose homes could house four or five families, do not live in castles. This, after all, is what makes it a metaphor. Presumably, the phrase applies to all sorts of homes: so-called

McMansions being constructed throughout the suburbs for the upper-middle class, the smallest homes found in urban and rural areas, and everything between.

Like all metaphors, the phrase reveals worlds beyond the obvious. If a man's home is his castle, then a man can't be simply a man. He must be the kind of man who befits a castle, who is worthy of the castle. A pauper? Certainly not. A prince? At least. Perhaps, as the other phrases in the epigraph suggest, he is a lord, even a king. This metaphor elevates common people—not one óf whom is a prince or princess, king or queen, many of whom are working stiffs living from paycheque to paycheque—to royalty. What comes with this metaphoric elevation? One important thing: height. Man here is metaphorically "raised up," moved from those ruled to those who rule from on high.[9] Whom does this lord or king rule? And why is height important?

The very words *lord* and *king* suggest and demand relationship with others. One cannot be a lord or king unless one has people over whom to rule. One cannot, really, be a lord unless one is acknowledged as such by other people.

Whom does the man in his castle rule? His spouse and children, of course. Since the man who is made metaphorical king has no literal subjects to rule, he must have metaphorical ones: his own family. Traditional wedding vows manifest this relationship between man and wife: she is to honour and obey. Children, traditionally, are to follow the rule of the father, who is the lord of the manor, the king of the castle. Outdated property and voting laws made this relationship manifest. Husbands, not wives, were allowed to own property and vote. The husband was, in theory, the voice of the family, its head. Why did this relationship work? Because society consented to it: the wife submitted to the husband, and the children were taught, and often forced, to submit to the mother and father.

The importance of others in establishing lordship and kingship is revealed in a very funny moment in Disney's wildly successful animated film *The Lion King*. After the lioness Nala has found the beatnik lion Simba slacking off in the jungle, she tries to convince him that he is king. The Pridelands, her home, his former home, suffers horribly under the tyrannous and maleficent rule of Scar, Simba's uncle. Scar assumed the throne after he killed Simba's father, Mufasa, and convinced Simba that Simba himself was responsible for Mufasa's death. At the centre of *The Lion King*, then, are these questions: Who killed Mufasa? The son? The uncle? Who should rule, or be the father to, the pride? The uncle? The son?

Simba believes that he was indeed responsible for his father's death and thus is not worthy to be his replacement. Simba believes that he is better off in the jungle with his friends, without other lions, without the chance, the hope, the burden of becoming a king and father.

It is significant that *The Lion King* portrays this segment of Simba's life as the life of the stereotypical beatnik of the 1950s and early 1960s. Simba has been raised by his friends, the meerkat Timon and the warthog Poomba, to reject responsibility, to turn his back on his lineage and to embrace an easy life of no worries. Simba has become a beat, rejecting his own destiny as father to the pride of lions, his role by birthright.

After refusing to take on Nala's challenge, Simba wanders dejectedly, berating his father for abandoning him. An encounter with the Shaman/Zen Master mandrill Rafiki changes his mind. With Rafiki's help, Simba finds his father again: Mufasa resides within Simba. This is a liberating moment: the son finds redemption by discovering that his father is present within himself. Simba had run away from the Pridelands because he thought he was responsible for his father's death. Now, he is made ready to return to the Pridelands in finding that his father's love for him is still present. Simba immediately rushes back to challenge the evil Scar and claim the throne. When Nala asks Rafiki if he knows where Simba is, Rafiki replies, "The king has returned."

Simba's surrogate family members, Timon and Poomba, follow (along with Nala). When they catch up with Simba, Poomba kneels before the young lion and declares his loyalty with this simple statement: "My liege." Thus, Poomba places himself in a subordinate role and makes Simba King. Simba is higher and Poomba is lower. Simba is the ruler; Poomba is the ruled. Simba's kingship depends on other's recognizing that his claim to kingship is valid.

Poomba's prostration also reminds us how important height is to the claims of kingship: the king is always higher than his subjects; the ideal castle is sited on high ground. The importance of height in ruling is reinforced by Simba's ascension to Pride Rock after he defeats Scar. Simba literally, and metaphorically, is above all the landscape and the animals that dwell therein. This is furthered by the image at the end of the film. Nala has given birth to a daughter; Rafiki appears to bless the cub and to hold it aloft on the top of Pride Rock, just as he had once held Simba high when he was a cub. As Rafiki holds the cub up, all the animals of the African plain—predators and prey, carnivores, herbivores and omnivores—bow down before the newborn, just as they had once bowed down before the newborn Simba. Already lower than the King of the Beasts, given Simba and his pride's perch on Pride Rock, they lower themselves even further: they scrape the ground in subservient homage to a baby that any one of them could easily kill.

Hidden in the joyous celebration of the return of the king is this irony: those very herbivores who bow to the king and the king's cub may well find their life forfeit to the king or his hunters. The lions need to eat, and they don't eat grass. Rather, as Simba's father once told him, they eat the animals that eat the grass. Granted, as Mufasa says, the lions eventually die and become soil that enriches the grass the herbivores eat, and so on. It is the great "circle of life." What Mufasa says is true, but is it liberating? Human ethical standards don't apply when non-human animals deal with each other. However, when animated animal tales are meant to serve as metaphorical explorations of the human condition, as they all are, then one must question their cosmologies. If one isn't the king, if one isn't a predator, if one isn't a carnivore, one gets eaten. Serfs in medieval England, after all, did not live to serve their own freedom; they lived to serve the freedom of their lords. As Timon says to Poomba when they first find Simba, broken and dying on the African plain, "Guys like him eat guys like us." Headship befits power, and power comes from height.

It is important to understand height because, in the cosmology of kingship, height moves the man, the husband and father, closer to the divine, to God. When Simba asks his father what the stars are, Mufasa tells him that they are the kings of old, looking down upon them. Indeed, Mufasa says that one day he will take his own place among the stars, watching Simba from above. Simba's rule is to be guided and validated by the pantheon of great kings who have assumed something of a divine place: they live among the stars and remain present to the king who is on earth. They guide him; his rule is validated not only by his subjects but also by these heavenly kings.

Non-animated kings have also traditionally claimed that their ruling height is guided by and validated by God. Indeed, in some cases kings claim to be, or are claimed to be, deities. Western European kings, for instance, long justified their own rule by divine right: God made them rulers in order to provide a secure and orderly commonwealth. The participation of the clergy—Roman Catholic or Protestant—in coronations and in the maintenance of the kings' power only supported this claim. Indeed, for a period of time, popes themselves were rulers of a nation state. Even today, Vatican City, small as it is, is a sovereign state: the pope is both spiritual leader of the Roman Catholic Church and the head of a secular state. Henry VIII's problems with siring a male heir were complicated because of his desire to maintain his divine validation: he wanted the Roman Catholic Church to approve his divorce so that he could marry within the Church. When the Church—led by the uncompromising Thomas More— did not approve, Henry had More killed. Henry then brought about the creation of his own national church—the Church of England—which approved his marriage and thus bestowed on him and his rule the sanction of God.

The Emperor of Japan took divine rights even further. Not content to be validated by God, the Emperor, supported by Japanese myth and culture, had long claimed that the Chrysanthemum throne was a direct manifestation of God. The Emperor, who called his country to battle in both World War I and World War II, was understood, metaphorically if not literally, to speak as God. It was not until the new Japanese constitution—forced on the Japanese by the American occupiers following World War II—that the Emperor lost divine status. Whether the ruler was European or Japanese, secular or religious, the pattern is clear: the height of the ruler moved him—and, in some cases, her—close to divinity, if not into divinity itself.

Thus, the phrase *a man's home is his castle* invokes metaphors that go beyond the obvious claim that the man's home, no matter how fancy or simple, is a castle. It suggests that the man is a lord or a king. It suggests that he rules over not only the castle but also the castle's inhabitants: traditionally, his spouse and children. It suggests that because of the height afforded by lordship and kingship, this man, this father, this ruler, is validated by, is guided by and is even identified with God. This connection between fathers and God has a long history, as the discussion below will show.

To understand the metaphors of father as thundergod and father as architect is to begin to understand ourselves at our deepest levels. Because these metaphors are deeply ingrained in the North American cultural narrative, one cannot understand that narrative's presentation of fathers without understanding these two metaphors: their presence and their problems.

This chapter contends that the metaphors of father as thundergod and father as architect are not agents of liberation. They do not, ultimately, help redeem or emancipate those involved with fathering. Father as thundergod is fundamentally oppressive and bombastic. Father as architect is distant. Both share one problem: they don't understand the lived worlds of their children and so they reject these worlds and, indeed, their children. In order to develop this claim, this chapter discusses the ways in which the North American cultural narrative has exposed the public and private problems with these metaphors, focusing on the animated film *Peter Pan*, the live-action film *Hook*, George Eliot's novel *Daniel Deronda*, James Baldwin's novel *Go Tell It on the Mountain*, and The Keys of the Kingdom, a series of novels for children. But first, we need to understand the theological and ideological roots of these metaphors.

The Lord, Zeus and the Dei

Thomas Laqueur offers a salient and concise entry into this difficult topic that is worth quoting. In his discussion of Sigmund Freud's *Moses and Monotheism*, Laqueur argues,

Here is the founding myth of the Father. "Paternity," Freud concludes, "is a supposition" and like belief in the Jewish God it is "based on an inference, a promise," while "maternity," like the old gods, is based on evidence of the senses alone. The invention of paternity, like that of a transcendent God, was thus also a "momentous step"; it likewise—Freud repeats the phrase but with a more decisive military emphasis—was a "conquest" of intellectuality over causality. (Laqueur, 1996, p. 178)

According to this reasoning, fathers are linked to divinity by act of the pure imagination unencumbered by material forces, by a move into the realm of idea over the realm of materiality. It is not news that many cultures that either predate the establishment of Jewish monotheism or are coincident with but uninfluenced it by it have female gods and divinities, often represented by the earth, breasts and wombs. Thus, when the Navajo, for instance, speak of Changing Woman and Mother Earth, they speak of a cosmology wholly different from that developed in the fertile river plains of the Middle East.

These maternal cultures deify women and women who give birth, who breastfeed, who create. The analogy is simple and profound. One observes woman pregnant, giving birth, breastfeeding. One observes female mammals pregnant, giving birth, nursing their young. One observes the earth pregnant in spring, giving birth, providing nourishment. Female is earth; earth is female. If we are born, who gives birth to us as humans? It must be a female divinity, for who else gives birth? This isn't to say that these cultures did not have male deities: they did. However, female—and, in particular, mother—imagery for the divine is profoundly present in these cultures, unlike in the Hebraic culture that eventually gave rise to Christianity and influenced the development of Islam. Hebraic culture eradicated the female god, the idea of the divine breast and womb, except within its own sub-cultures that erupted from time to time, as in some of the female Christian mystics of medieval Europe. The Hebraic culture opted, as Freud suggests, for "intellectuality" over "causality." It broke the material analogy that linked women to the gods through pregnancy and birth. It posited that there is a God who creates, but that this creation takes place not through the sweat and blood of matter but through lan-guage and the mind. Thus, in the creation story that opens the Bible (Genesis 1–2:4b), God creates by speaking: the divine seems relatively distant from the created order, so much so that God gives humans sovereignty over it.

This, indeed, is the first seed of God as both thunder-god and architect. God speaks from on high: "Let there be light!" Once God has created through the thunderous word, he exits the created order, giving it over to humans. It is as if God says, "It is your building now. Follow my design." God does reappear from time to time in the Hebrew Bible, but does so as a thundergod. When God is disgusted with humans, he floods the earth with rain, killing all but the select. Granted, God feels remorse and promises Noah that he shall never again smite the earth with rain, but the dam-age is done: God has already acted thunderously. When God speaks to Moses on Sinai, God speaks thunderously. Moses, understandably, trembles before the divine presence and asks, "Who are you?" God replies, "I am who I am (or "I will be who I will be")" (Exodus 3). God then emerges as a war god, smiting enemies and even, on occasion, his own people. God sends the angel of death to kill the firstborn of Egypt, an act of revenge and retribution in response to the Egyptians' slaying of the firstborn of the Hebrews. God appears as a whirlwind to slow the advancing Egyptian army. God then lures the Egyptian troops into the valley of the parted Red Sea and kills them all, thunderously releasing the raging torrent of water upon the heads of the oppressors. And so it goes.

Laqueur's discussion of Freud's *Moses and Monotheism* reminds us to consider both the metaphors that are used to describe the ascension of the father and the father God, and the ways in which the idea of transcendence is linked to these metaphors. Freud tells us that the ascension of the father and the father God is a triumph, a conquest. Thus Freud invokes and reinforces the link between the father and the father God and what is the core of military activity (on the whole, the province of the male): violence and war. To say that the ascension of the father and the father God over the mother and the mother God is a triumphant conquest is to suggest that these fathers and mothers and father Gods and mother Gods were at war. Today we speak of the "battle of the sexes." This military metaphor suggests that men and women are opposing armies battling for dominance.

As the ascendant God, the father God is transcendent: a God who defies the limitations of time and space and has claim over all time and all space. Thus the Hebrews justify their conquest of "the land of milk and honey" by their claim that Palestine was promised to them by their father God who is the father God of all time and all space. This father God has given birth to all, and his preferred children, the Hebrews, have claim to it. Thus the Christian missionaries justify their conquest of the new world by their claim that their father God is the father God of all. The father God is transcendent and, so it appears, validates triumphant conquest.

As the father God waxes, the mother Gods wane. Thus, fatherhood waxes and motherhood wanes. Thus, the mind waxes and the body wanes. Thus, the "idea" waxes and "materiality" wanes. As Laqueur holds (as did Simone de Beauvoir before him in her 1949 landmark study of woman, *The Second Sex: Woman as Other*), motherhood is presumed to be a fact because of the fact of the uterus: women can be seen to be pregnant, can be seen to birth the child, can be seen to feed the child. Fatherhood, in contrast, is presumed to be an idea: fathers are not involved in the materiality of the baby's life in the ways in which mothers are. They may impregnate, thus helping women create life, but are not tied down to that life that they helped create. Fathers may transcend the local, material conditions to which mothers are bound. Once a woman is pregnant, she cannot be impregnated again until that pregnancy comes to its end. Of course, the very language with which we speak about such matters demonstrates they way we consent to this vision of the triumphant conquest of the father. The mother is impregnated; the father impregnates. The mother is acted upon; the father acts. The father, indeed, may impregnate many women nearly simultaneously: he is, other than by convention and culture, bound to none. Is this natural, the way it has to be? The point of this book is to suggest that the answer to this question is no.

As Laqueur argues, the fact of motherhood, based on our interpretation of the presence of the womb in women, denigrates mothers because materiality itself has been denigrated in Western culture in favour of the non-material, the ideal (Laqueur, 1996, pp. 175–179). Graven images of the gods, for instance, were forbidden early in the development of monotheism, which was a male phenomenon. This God was named as male: as father, as lord, as king. Thus, when the Hebrews, desperately wandering in the desert following their escape from Egypt, constructed a graven image in order to find hope, it is destroyed by the Lord and by his representative, Moses.

Powerful developments in feminist theology notwithstanding, we live in a culture in which fathers and God are intimately intertwined: our predominant image of God is that of a father and king; our fathers often are made into gods and kings, literally and metaphorically. God rules and so do fathers. God leads and so do fathers. God has power and so do fathers. As Merry Weisner-Hanks argues,

> Fatherhood ... has been linked to ... the exercise of power in both real and metaphorical terms. The words for "father" and leader are etymologically related in many languages, and the male originators of institutions and structures were often labeled "fathers"—the church fathers, the

founding fathers. Hereditary monarchs such
as kings, emperors, and tsars were praised
as the fathers of their people and used
paternal language in their attempts to build
or maintain their own power. (Weisner-
Hanks, 2001, p. 101)

Ralph LaRossa reminds us that in colonial America,
"Fatherhood had deep ties to Christianity and its patriarchal
tenets. Thus, like God the father, men as fathers were expected to be both loving and just; and they were religiously
bound to be authority figures in the home" (LaRossa, 1997,
p. 25).

The Roman Catholic Church's continuous refusal to
entertain the idea that women might become priests is part
of this intertwined history of God and fathers. Proponents
of the argument that women should be ordained as priests
claim that Jesus' vision was inclusive of both men and
women. Opponents argue that although Jesus' vision was
inclusive, men are best able to represent it as priests. After
all, Jesus was a man, the twelve apostles were men, and God
is a father.

God and fathers are linked in ways that are impossible
to deny, difficult to unlink. For us, living in the midst of the
North American cultural narrative, this link plays out in
many ways, two of the most prominent being thundergod
and architect.

Father as thundergod and father as architect are theological cousins, linked to different understandings of God as
they have developed. Father as thundergod resonates with

both the presentation of the Lord in some parts of the He-brew Bible and with the presentation of Zeus in the Greek myths. Both the Lord and Zeus were understood to be male deities, fathers of the earth and its inhabitants. Both also were gods of thunder, speaking powerfully from the mystery of their beings. They were involved with their charges, but weren't particularly nurturing. They demanded obedience, gave commands and felt free to smite both their enemies and their own people when necessary. (Of course, this is not the whole story. Both the Lord and Zeus have other character-istics: "motherly" ones, even. The Book of Isaiah describes the Lord in nurturing terms, and Zeus provides a "womb" of sorts for his unborn son Dionysus when the child's mortal mother is provoked by a jealous Hera into forcing Zeus to reveal himself in all his godly splendour. She is immediately incinerated. Zeus rescues the child from her womb and sews him into a pocket of skin on his thigh, carrying him until he can be born.) Father as architect resonates with deistic conceptions of God: the being who constructed the earth, endowed it and its inhabitants with natural law, and then rested, forever, out of the play of earthly affairs. While this God allows for freedom of a sort, he doesn't, because he can't, act beyond the "first cause": he gave up his agency when the building was complete.

Fathers as Architects: Public and Private

A recent series of children's novels consciously calls to our attention this architectural understanding of the divinity. Five of the projected seven novels in The Keys to the Kingdom series have been published as of 2007: *Mister Monday*, *Grim Tuesday*, *Drowned Wednesday*, *Sir Thursday* and *Lady Friday*. The series details the problems at The House and its seven attendant spaces. The House and these spaces are ultimately the province of the "architect," the creative power of being itself: the House is thus responsible not only for itself but also for all of the realities of existence. If all is right with the House, all is right with all of existence.

The problem? All is not right with the House. There is disorder verging on chaos: the centre of existence itself is beginning to crumble. Why? The architect is nowhere to be found and thus cannot assert her creative power over the centre of being and all other manifestations of being, including that planet called Earth. Earth's problems, as a mortal, temporal realm, are directly related to the disorder found at the centre of being, the House.

The architect left the House and, when she did so, she divided her realm into seven spaces. She gave control of the seven spaces to lesser beings—all were powerful, but none were as powerful as she. They were to form a council to manage the House and thus all of existence, according the original plan. Each controls not only one of the seven spaces but also a segment of time: one of the days of the week. However, each of the guardians, in his or her own way, has become corrupt and power hungry, to the detriment of the House and all of existence. In that corrupt state, each represents and manifests a traditional vice. Mistress Wednesday, for instance, takes the form of a whale as she controls the eternal seas. She also controls Wednesday as it exists across all of reality. In her corruption she has become a glutton, devouring massive amounts of food. She is constantly hungry, never satiated.

Called into help the House regain order is a boy from Earth, auspiciously named Arthur. He must gain possession of the "keys" that control the seven spaces. When Arthur has all seven keys, he will be able to bring order to the House and thus all of existence. Garth Nix, the books' author, has clearly and deftly named for a new generation of young people the metaphor of the architect who creates and then exits. Granted, he does so with a twist: the architect is called "she." Nix thus takes the traditional idea of the father God and inverts it. The divine power is feminine, but with traditional male characteristics: she creates, orders and leaves.

It is important to note here the fundamental difference between the deadbeat and the architect. The deadbeat creates and leaves, but does not particularly care about the emotional or physical well-being and welfare of his creation. The architect, on the other hand, does care. In the case of the architect in The Keys to the Kingdom books, she creates with care and with conscious attention to order. The problem is that she then steps away and leaves others to take over the beloved creation. Little does she know that these guardians will create chaos and threaten all of existence.

Some of the most famous literary examples of the father as architect are found in the novels of Jane Austen. One need only think of the father of the brood of girls in *Pride and Prejudice* to understand fully this metaphor. Mr. Bennet certainly acts as God: his wife and daughters need his implicit or explicit permission to act. For instance, when a Mr. Bingley leases a mansion in the Bennet's part of the country, Mrs. Bennet is keen to make her family known to him. Why? Because he is young, rich and single and she has five daughters to marry off. She dreams of one them making a marriage with this newcomer, even though she has never met him. Youth and money go a long way in a social order driven by profitable marriage contracts. Although Mr. Bennet assures Mrs. Bennet that she can take her daughters to meet Mr. Bingley herself (Austen, 2003, p. 2)—because he certainly has no intention of doing so—she knows she cannot, given the context of the society of the landed gentry of late 18th-century England. It would be unseemly and improper for Mrs. Bennet and her daughters to call on Mr. Bingley without the mediation of a husband and father. Fortunately for Mrs. Bennet and his daughters, Mr. Bennet does introduce himself to Mr. Bingley, thus setting into motion a whole series of events, most of which concern courting.

Mr. Bennet is thus present in the lives of his daughters, but scarcely so. Interestingly, however, when Mr. Bingley first calls on the Bennets, he meets only with Mr. Bennet, in Mr. Bennet's favourite retreat, the library (6). Mr. Bingley has heard about the beautiful Bennet daughters and hopes to see them. He sits only with the father, however, as decorum dictates. It would appear here that Mr. Bennet is a thundergod, as the father who rules all from on high, dictating the lives of his wife and daughters.

This image quickly passes, however, once the connection with Mr. Bingley is established. Mr. Bennet essentially retreats, preferring his library and the world of books to active participation in the lives of his family. For instance, he chooses not to attend the first dance at which Mr. Bingley meets the Bennet daughters, a dance at which two streams of the novel emerge. In the first, Mr. Bingley and the eldest Bennet daughter, Jane, dance, spark and begin to fall in love. In the second, Mr. Bennet's second and favourite daughter, Elizabeth, encounters Mr. Bingley's good friend Mr. Darcy, the man whom she will love to hate and then love to love.

Why did Mr. Bennet send his girls and his wife off to this fateful dance, choosing not accompany them? He favoured his library and a book (9): he was content enough to see them go and know that they would return. Mr. Bennet does not want to be involved with or even hear about the intimate details of his family's life.

He is content to spend his time in his study, distant from the affairs of his household. With his wife, he created the world of his house, but he wants little to do with it. He doesn't abandon his children, yet he leaves them to themselves, allowing them to figure out their own lives and loves as they will.

He has not provided for his daughters' financial futures, and takes no active role in finding them suitable husbands.

As the narrative develops, others do what Mr. Bennet, the fatherly architect, cannot. They take care of his house.

When his youngest daughter, Lydia, runs off with a disreputable man, it is not her father but her uncle and Mr. Darcy who take responsibility and arrange for the two to marry. Mr. Bennet watches, aware, but does not interfere.

One fatherly character in the North American cultural narrative that doesn't even watch his family is one Peter Banning in the feature film *Hook*. The movie is a "what-if" film: what if Peter Pan actually left Neverland? The film tells us that Peter continued to visit Wendy, even as she grew up, married and had children of her own. He returns one night to find Wendy as a grandmother. He takes one look at her granddaughter, Moira, and decides then and there that he will give her a kiss. It is not the thimble, that metaphoric kiss of innocence that he shared with Wendy in the original *Peter Pan*, but rather a real kiss. Once he does so, he cannot return to Neverland. Apparently, his link to Neverland was a lack of sexual awareness: once he enters the dangerous and mysterious world of sexuality, he is forever banned from the magical place somewhere beyond the second star on the right.

Wendy has grown up to be a benefactress, working on behalf of orphaned children. She arranges for Peter (who is still a boy) to be adopted by American parents. Eventually, he marries Moira. They have children together, but Peter proves to be a classic architect of a father. He provides well for his family, lives with them, and even loves them after a fashion. But he is more dedicated to his career, to making money in mergers and acquisitions, than he is to the lives of his children.

As the movie opens, his daughter is performing in an elementary school stage version of *Peter Pan*, and Peter, with Moira and son Jack, is in the audience. During the song "I Won't Grow Up," Peter receives a business call on his cell phone. He takes the call, does business and misses the play. Moreover, he schedules a meeting for the next day, at exactly the time that his son is going to play in the most important little league baseball game of his career. Peter promises Jack that he will be at the game, saying, "My word is my bond."

His word proves to be worthless. Instead of going to the game, he sends one of his employees to videotape it. The employee is able to tape the last out, where Jack strikes out to end the game. Peter arrives at the field only after the teams have left. This sets the stage for what follows: a return trip to London to celebrate a hospital wing being named after Wendy, to honour her work on behalf of orphans. While on the plane trip over, Jack draws a picture of the plane crashing. Four figures float in the air next to the burning plane. Three have parachutes: Mom Moira, sister Wendy, son Jack. The fourth figure doesn't: Peter, the father, is doomed to die.

If *Peter Pan,* the play and the animated Disney film, is about mothers and children, *Hook* is about fathers and children. *Peter Pan* centres on Wendy: her role as storyteller and older sister and quasi-mother to John and Michael, her younger brothers, and her role as mother to the lost boys in Neverland. The Disney version of *Peter Pan* has Peter admonish the lost boys for trying to kill Wendy, upon Tinker

Bell's insistence. Tinker Bell is jealous of Peter's relationship with Wendy and wants her dead. (This is what leads to the scene in *Hook* in which Tinker Bell kisses Peter, making public her latent sexual desire for him.) The lost boys trust Tinker Bell, and the animated film shows them attacking Wendy with energy and gusto. Peter saves her from crashing horribly and immediately calls the lost boys to attention. They expect to be congratulated for their heroism. Instead, they receive a withering condemnation. Peter savages them for trying to kill the mother he has brought to them. They are shocked: "Mother?" They then welcome Wendy into their lives: she is the mother they have all lost, the mother they have all dreamed about. Like Wendy's mother, Wendy emerges as the caring figure in their lives: the one who will tell them stories. They come to care for her so much that they, following her lead, abandon Peter: they choose to leave Neverland with their new mother. Peter is important to them, but the mother is more so. In *Hook*, this vision of the mother continues: the mother is stable, secure, nurturing. Moira is present, active, caring.

The father, in contrast, is absent: Peter is father as architect. Interestingly, the only father figure in Disney's *Peter Pan* is a bellowing thundergod: Mr. Darling is a pompous blowhard who yells at and viciously mimics his children. The film opens with John and Michael battling: John is Captain Hook; Michael is Peter Pan. The father walks in on the scene looking for his cuff links and front plate for his suit: he and Mrs. Darling are on their way to a formal event. The cuff links are treasure in the boys' play; the front plate is a treasure map. The father, incensed, yells at his sons for taking his things; he yells at Wendy for telling them the stories that lead them to desecrate his things; he yells at the dog for making him fall. He declares that these stories about Peter Pan are nonsense and that Wendy may no longer stay in the nursery with the boys. With pontificating power, he declares that she must grow up. Wendy is shocked, hurt, tearful. Her mother comforts her and attempts to soothe the thunder-god, but he will not be moved. As Mr. Darling walks away from the house, he mocks Peter Pan and Captain Hook and thus mocks his children's love of these characters as well.

In contrast, the father in *Hook*, Peter himself, is an architect, not a thundergod. He has helped to create a family but then has exited from its life. Moreover, he has competition from an unlikely source: his arch-enemy, Captain Hook. Hook, who has a score to settle with Peter, kidnaps Peter's children to lure him back to Neverland.

Jack, suffering from Peter's absence in his life, is attracted to the Captain. Hook seduces Jack: he offers him care, concern and attention, all the while pointing out Peter's failings as a father. He even goes so far as to arrange a baseball game in which Jack can star. Jack can't help himself. He joins with the captain, going so far as to dress like him: he becomes a miniature Hook.

The significance of this narrative move—Jack playing baseball with pirates—cannot be underestimated. Baseball, as "America's national pastime," is a particularly important part of the relationship between fathers and sons, or so the American cultural narrative tells us. It is replete with images of fathers, sons and baseball. What does Dad place in his infant son's crib? A baseball mitt and ball. Who takes his son to the baseball game? Dad. Who plays catch in the backyard? Father and son. Baseball has long served as a metaphorical and literal bond between father and son in America. A colleague of mine once told me that she never fails to be moved when she sees a father and son together at a baseball game.

Moreover, baseball is, at its foundation, a game. While professional baseball is undeniably a business, and while over-involved little league parents sometimes turn the kids' version of the game into a violent slugfest, baseball is really about play, just as pretending to be pirates is about play. Baseball offers Jack, as it does many boys and girls, the opportunity to enter into a game whose rules have nothing to do with school, homework or cleaning one's room. Baseball is a fantasy, like playing pirates is fantasy. One dresses in a costume, one enters into another reality marked by roles that don't exist in the real world.. Viewers likewise enter into a fantasy, a carnival of sorts. They cheer, they moan, they eat copious amounts of food and drink, letting the normal concerns of their normal lives slip away, if only for a couple of hours.

Captain Hook, devilish genius that he is, knows that there are many ways to defeat Peter. One is to defeat him with a sword, which he wants to do. Another way is to defeat him as a father, which he wants to do as well. If he is to become Jack's surrogate father, stepping into the void left by Peter, he must engage Jack in Jack's world, in Jack's deepest desires. Captain Hook arranges a game between two teams whose players, except for one, are his pirates. The one exception is Jack.

So, Jack is able to enter into what must be an extraordinary fulfillment of his fantasy life: he plays baseball and pirates simultaneously. Needless to say, Jack is the star. With Hook watching him and cheering for him, Jack hits a home run. The surrogate father-to-be, Hook, is able to cheer for Jack in Jack's glory. This contrasts with Peter, who had been unable to commiserate with Jack earlier in the story when Jack struck out. When Jack hits the home run, Hook is delighted, as is Jack.

Less delighted is Peter, who has hidden himself under the bleachers to watch the game. Peter understands what is transpiring: he is losing his son to Hook because Hook attends to Jack in a way that Peter never has. Although Hook undoubtedly has ulterior motives—he wants to battle Peter one last time and is using Jack as leverage (he did kidnap him, after all)—Jack doesn't fully understand this. In his captivity he has come to identify with his captor because his captor appears to care for him. All Jack knows is that his own father, while present in his life, is not fully present. He has not entered his children's lives, their lives of play, as Moira tells him. Peter is "into" his work, but not his children. He has left Jack's life to Moira and to assistants who videotape his failures. Hook, on the other hand, attends to Jack fully.

In the case of both Mr. Bennet and Peter, the effects of their fatherly indifference are largely private, although the private does spill over into the public. Neither narrative deals with the grand problems of the public realm: government, war, peace, hunger, morality, religion and the like. Rather, both are fundamentally about families: how they are shaped and threatened. This is not surprising. After all, in neither case are we talking about the metaphorical fathers of nations, churches or states. We are talking about fathers of families.

And yet, each narrative does indicate the ways in which the private and public have permeable boundaries. It is not the case that the "private is the public," as some feminists suggest (see Gavison 1992 for an overview). It is the case, however, that the private and public are connected. As polar opposites, they need each other, influence each other. Take *Pride and Prejudice*. Mr. Bennet's inability and unwillingness to involve himself fully in the lives of his daughters results in Lydia's wildness, which leads her to run away with Mr. Wickham, regardless of the effect this action will have on her family. Part of the effect is private: her parents and siblings are concerned about her and her welfare. Part of the effect is public. Elizabeth knows, and others confirm, that people of their station (i.e. gentlemen) will not want to be associated with the family that produced such a daughter and is tainted by scandal. Thus, Mr. Bennet's inattention leads to a situation in which his peers will ostracize his daughters. If one of his duties is to arrange for profitable marriages for his girls, he is failing miserably.

The realm of the private intersects with the realm of the public in *Hook* as well. Peter's inattention to his children creates a situation in which they are physically and psychically vulnerable. Captain Hook takes advantage of this vulnerability. First, he kidnaps the children. Peter, having forgotten that he has a mortal enemy who might someday take revenge, leaves his children unprotected. Second,

Hook psychically kidnaps Jack. The physical and psychic kidnapping of the children has very public consequences, at least for Neverland. Peter has to return, rediscover that he is "the Pan," and fight Hook to the death. Does it all work out for the best? Of course. It is a Hollywood film, after all, and a Hollywood film about a beloved figure in the cultural narrative's pantheon. Still, Peter's private actions, seemingly confined to his family, had enormous public effect.

◎   ◎   ◎

Fathers as Thundergods: Public and Private

So, too, the thundergod's actions, at least as they are depicted in parts of the North American cultural narrative, begin in the privacy of family life but move into the public. If the architect creates the order of the world only to leave it largely to its own devices, the thundergod is imperiously present, launching bolts of lightning, thunderous words, divine commands and pronouncements from on high.

A perfect vision of the father as thundergod is revealed in *Daniel Deronda*. Perhaps not surprisingly, this father as thundergod is Jewish, allowing George Eliot to tap into the culture's understanding of the Lord: the God who creates through pronouncement; who commands Abraham to sacrifice his own son in order to prove his loyalty; who floods his own world when he is too disgusted with it to stand the sight of it; who kills an entire generation of Egyptian children as revenge; who commands the world. In *Daniel*

Deronda, this thundergod is Daniel Deronda's maternal grandfather.

Toward the end of the novel, Daniel is summoned to meet his mother, whom he does not remember, and whom he has not seen since he was toddler. She is dying and wishes to see the son she gave to Sir Hugo Mallinger, who loved her so much that he was willing to take on her son so that she might have the freedom to build a career as a singer. She wanted her freedom more than she wanted a new husband, more even than she wanted her son (Eliot, 2003, p. 634).

Daniel Deronda was written in 1876, when the rights of women were first beginning to be discussed publicly in Europe and America. Daniel's mother serves as metaphor for women who were trying to understand and overcome their subservient lives within the context of an oppressive patriarchal order. For Daniel's mother, that means trying to understand and overcome her life as the daughter of an orthodox Jewish father, a father who believed in what some in our own era call "traditional family values." That is to say, the family follows a certain order in which the father rules and the children, especially the female children, obey.

Daniel's grandfather was a highly educated man, but a man devoted to a particular understanding of the world. He belonged to his "people," and his people belonged to the Lord. As such, he raised his daughter to be obedient to that tradition, which was to her no more than a "thunder without meaning" in her ears (630). This quotation is key. The Lord speaks thunderously to Moses and the prophets; they, in turn, speak thunderously to the chosen people. The fathers of the chosen people—following the male lineage of Abraham, Isaac, Jacob, Moses and the prophets—speak thunderously to their children.

Daniel's grandfather told his mother what she could and couldn't be. She "wanted to live a large life, with freedom to do what everyone else did" (630). By "everyone else" she means, in particular, men. She tells Daniel how hard it was to be a woman with a drive and genius equal to any man's in a family and culture that would not allow her to express that drive and freedom. Her father, in particular, would not hear of it. Instead, he treated her like the Jewish woman he wanted her to be. She was to marry, to have sons, to be a link between himself and his male progeny, delivered through the intermediary of his daughter's body (631, 634).

The effect of the father's thunder was devastating. He created a situation in which his daughter felt forced to give up her son so that she might be free. He created a situation in which his grandson was raised well but always with a feeling of loss: he was without a mother and father. To be sure, Daniel became free in ways that could not have been imagined. He became an amalgam of Judaism and Christianity, of the bourgeois tradition of the English gentleman and the messianic tradition of Hebraic thought. Daniel emerges as the new Adam, and Mirah, Daniel's wife, emerges as the new Eve. However, he emerges thus only because his mother abandoned him, only because he was raised lovingly but always in lack.

The father as thundergod is not limited to nineteenth-century narratives about orthodox Jewish patriarchs, as James Baldwin's *Go Tell It on the Mountain* demonstrates. As we saw in chapter 2, Gabriel abandons his first son, both financially and psychically, and the boy's life ends early and violently. When given a second chance at fatherhood, through adoption and biology, Gabriel changes his practice. No longer is he deadbeat: instead, he becomes thundergod, much to his family's detriment.

Gabriel's link to God is even clearer than that of Daniel Deronda's maternal grandfather. Gabriel, as a young man, became well known as a preacher in the South; he had a powerful voice and a powerful presence. People understood him to be one of God's anointed, a man to be listened to. Indeed, Gabriel had a vision in which God promised him that his descendants, like those of Abraham, would rise in glory with the help of the Lord (Baldwin, 1952, p. 112). Even in his later life, once he had abandoned the South and moved to Harlem, he was head deacon in the Temple of the Fire Baptized (12). Gabriel is a holy man.

But within the privacy of his family life, he is domineering and abusive. He abuses his children verbally and physically. Why? Because he loves them, at least according to their mother, Elizabeth (23). Roy, Gabriel's second biological son (named after his first son, Royal, and Gabriel's vision), hates the abuse, likening it to being beaten like a dog (23). Roy wants no part of this love, or the church and God linked to it. He loves his mother; that much is clear. He appreciates their relationship as much as he hates the relationship he has with his father: "Tell me how come he don't never let me talk to him like I talk to you? He's my father, ain't he? But he don't never listen to me—no, I all the time got to listen to him" (25).

Elizabeth clearly is the nurturing presence in the material lives of her children: she feeds them, clothes them, talks to them. Gabriel, in contrast, commands with fists and shouts. Elizabeth's only defence is classic: "Your father ... knows best" (25). *Go Tell It on the Mountain* was first published in 1952, when the phrase "father knows best" was in the air. Just as Hollywood offered its own white, suburban version of that adage, Baldwin, writing from the perspective of the black underclass, presented his own.

Gabriel's vision, that he will raise a son who would be glorified by the Lord, is an illusion. Royal, the first biological son, does not have a glorious end. Roy, the second biological son, follows in his long-dead half-brother's footsteps. Soon after the conversation with his mother, Roy ends up with a knife wound, earned in a gang fight with some whites. At first, Gabriel's reaction is tender. He tends to Roy's wound and "muttered sweet, delirious things to Roy" as he wipes the blood from his head.

At this moment, Gabriel is neither deadbeat nor thundergod, but a tender and loving father, incarnate in the material world of his children.

It doesn't last, however. Gabriel soon thunders at Elizabeth, blaming her for Roy's wounds. He shouts that it is she who is responsible for the children's care while he is out of the house earning money (47). Rather than taking responsibility himself, or holding Roy accountable, he blames the wife and mother. When she defends herself, he becomes outraged and slaps her so hard that she falls, crumbling under his power (48). Roy rises to his mother's defence: "Don't you slap my mother. That's my *mother*. You slap her again, you black bastard, and I swear to God I'll kill you" (48). Thus Gabriel has created a situation in which Roy is raised in violence and offers violence in return. Roy is neither redeemed nor emancipated; he is wild and is willing to exact violent revenge on his violent father. The beloved son has risen against the father in defence of the mother, as sons have always done.

Roy's reaction to Gabriel is part of the Western, if not the global, narrative trajectory. When the father as thundergod harms the person the child holds most dear, the father is challenged.

Unfortunately for all, the thundergod can only thunder. Gabriel can't enter into the reality of either of his sons' lives. He can't work for their liberation because he sees only what he thought God promised him, sees only what he wants, what he desires.

5

The Fool

"Let me give you my wife; she's in charge."

—husbands everywhere

Images

1

Since I was on sabbatical and had no one but myself to report to, to answer to, I scheduled myself to pick up my four-year-old daughter at her school and take her to her annual well-child physical. When my wife left in the early morning for her day at work, she reminded me.

"You're taking her to the doctor?"

"Yes," I said, smiling.

"*Don't forget to pack her some snacks. She won't be able to eat a snack at school because you'll have to pick her up before snack time, and she'll be hungry. Bring her something to drink and something to eat.*"

I grinned and said, jokingly, "*I'm not a complete incompetent.*"

"*I know. I know.*" *She left, probably thinking, if only sub-consciously, what does he know?*

@ @ @

Images
2

"*Why did you buy these?*" *she asked, trying hard to maintain an even tone.*

"*What?*"

"*These vitamins. You'll have to cut them in half. One tablet is meant for an adult, not a child.*"

"*Ah. I didn't read the label.*"

"*Do you want to cut them in half?*"

"*I don't care.*"

"*Why didn't you just buy the kind she likes?*"

"*Uhhh ...*"

"Ah." She shook her head, smiled a half-smile, the right side of her mouth rising, and walked away.

◎　◎　◎

He Tries Hard

As the previous chapter has established, the North American cultural narrative has soundly criticized metaphorical fathers and thus, implicitly, real fathers, for acting as thundergods or architects.

If pedophiles and deadbeats are, by definition, unacceptable metaphorical models for fatherhood, if thundergods and architects have been rejected by the North American cultural narrative, what is left? The father as fool. Coincident with its exploration of and rejection of thundergods and architects, the cultural narrative of the 20th century began to explore and reject, and indeed continues to explore and reject, the father as fool. Why? If thundergods have been removed from Olympus, if architects have been ripped away from their drafting tables, fathers had to go somewhere. They went, at least in one strand of the cultural narrative, into the home. The gods came down and entered the human world. The architects came to inhabit the spaces they had created. However, these new dads are pathetic, in the fundamental meaning of that word: they elicit pathos because they are fools. Fallen thundergods and architects, one strand of the cultural narrative would have us understand, don't do well in the home. They are a source of comedy.

This metaphor of the fool is not the Dostoevskian holy fool, that figure who reveals to us the sinfulness of our own existence and the possibility of God's liberating activity. Would that it were so. The holy fool is an honourable metaphor, one that some fathers might gladly take on as their own, as a model for fatherly behaviour.

After all, it is better to be a fool on a divine errand than to be a fool, plain and simple. However, the North American cultural narrative has not provided metaphoric fathers who are divine fools, revealing to the world the error of its blindness, the possibility of liberation. Rather, it has provided metaphoric fathers who are plain fools, revealing to the world that fathers are incompetents. The North American cultural narrative's presentation of the father as fool is informed by, and informs, real life. This brings us back to the epigraph that begins this chapter:

"Let me give you my wife. She's in charge."

This statement, a metaphor drawn from commonplace culture, says that men not only can't dictate a schedule, they can't even set it. They must turn to their wives, their children's mothers, who are the bosses, the captains. As fools, fathers provide comic relief, but they can't substantially contribute to the liberation of their children, themselves, or their partner. Mainly, they exist as foils for their children and their wives: they illuminate how wise their wives are, how competent their children are. The father, in a fundamental sense, is infantile.

This epigraph emerged from a conversation about children's schedules. I once called the house of a friend of his son to see whether the friend could come and spend the night. The father who called could have immediately asked for the mother.

"Hi. Is Jane home? My son wants to invite your son over to spend the night, and I'd like to see if he can come."

This would have been insulting, although true to life and more efficient. Instead, the conversation went something like this:

"Hi. My son wants to invite your son over to spend the night. Is he free?"

"Let me give you my wife; she's in charge."

The epigraph reveals a strange metaphoric tension of control. The first grammatical sentence, to the left of the semi-colon, suggests that the husband and father is in charge. When he says, "Let me give you my wife" he invokes a commonplace phrase, variations of which we use all the time. It suggests that the speaker controls the other and that the other can be given by the speaker to the person who has initiated the conversation. However, the second grammatical sentence, that to the right of the semi-colon, belies the import of the first. The wife, the mother, is in charge.

What is it to be in charge? Two possibilities exist. First, the mother is a military leader, able to order her troops to charge. She commands her underlings, her subordinates: children and husband. The husband and father is, at best, a lieutenant or senior non-commissioned officer. He can make some decisions, presumably, but true command authority resides higher up the chain, with the commander, who is the wife and mother. This metaphor invokes the classic dialectic of higher and lower. As the one who is in command, she is higher than the ones over whom she has charge; they are lower. Second, this metaphor suggests that the mother controls the energy of the household. In this case, to be in charge is to be in control of the power: she can distribute it or not, as she wishes. This metaphor invokes the classic dialectic of centre and periphery, or beginning and end. She is at the centre or the beginning of the energy circuit: she sends and the others receive. In either case, the father is revealed to be one of the troops, one of the receivers. He does not command the family. He does not send energy to them.

The images that begin this chapter also point to the position of father as fool. In the first, my wife, the mother of my children, reveals that she doesn't trust me to care competently for their children. However many times I might make them breakfast, lunch and dinner; however much I might comfort them, bathe them, play with them; however many times I might help them dress, help them with their homework, help them ride a bike; however much I might care for them, she can't finally trust me to get the job done in a way that meets her approval. She is the supervisor. I am the supervised. She is the commanding officer. I am the subordinate. She is the energy centre. I am a transfer station. She is in charge. Why? Because she thinks I am a fool.

Her conclusion is not without reason. The second image that begins this chapter involves the same people. Once again, I prove to her that she can't quite trust me with our children's lives and health. While it is true that I ran an errand for the family, saving her from having to do it, I failed. Why? Because I didn't read. I acted like the village idiot.

"May I help you, sir?" the pharmacist asked.

"Uh ... I need vitamins. For my daughter. Yeah."

"You'll find them in Aisle 10."

These, I take these, I said to myself, grabbing the first package of chewable vitamins I could find.

Again, I amaze her. It is not unlike the times I have to ask whether or not my daughter's and my wife's pink clothes should be washed with darks or lights. There I am, doing the laundry, but I am not really trustworthy because I am a fool. *How many times do I have to tell him that pink is always a light?* she asks herself.

Fool, Defined

Simpleton. Dolt. Dunce. Blockhead. Numbskull. Ignoramus. Dunderhead. Ninny. Nincompoop. Booby. Saphead. Sap. All of these are synonyms for fool; none leaves its meaning ambiguous. Four of them—blockhead, numbskull, dunderhead and saphead—speak directly to the issue, albeit metaphorically. The fool has something wrong with his or her head. Of course, in the case of this chapter, it is "his" alone.

The comic strip character Charlie Brown is perhaps the most famous blockhead in the North American cultural narrative. Lovable but foolish: that is Charlie Brown. Time after time, he allows himself to be tricked by Lucy: she promises to hold the football so that he can kick it, but always pulls it away at the last moment so that he flies into the air, landing flat on his back. Time after time, he flies a kite in spring, only to have the kite-eating tree devour it. Time after time, he hopes that his love for the little red-haired girl will be requited, but it never is. To a certain extent, Charlie Brown is a Dostoevskian fool: we are meant to read in his foolishness profound statements about the human condition. Still, he is a blockhead, as Lucy calls him. Why else would he let himself be tricked over and over again?

If Charles Schultz had created a comic strip featuring his characters as adults, Charlie Brown, save an extraordinary personality transformation, would be a foolish father. Chuck could never be a pedophile or a deadbeat: after all, who would syndicate, let alone read, such a comic strip? He could never be a thundergod. What thundergod is "wishy-washy"? (Lucy could be a thundergod, if we were discussing mothers: Lucy would be the female, motherly equivalent to Zeus.) Nor could Chuck be an architect: he would want to be too involved, too much part of his children's lives to stand aloof, removed, distant. After all, this is the boy who purchased a nearly dead Christmas tree in the Charlie Brown Christmas special, forever revealing his tender, concerned side. No, Chuck would be a fool, a fool wanting to show his kids how to fly kites, wanting to fly kites with his kids, only to lose his, and theirs, to the kite-eating tree.

It is significant, though, that Charlie Brown would want to fly kites with his kids. It is this desire to be involved, to be part of the material lives that their children lead, that brings all foolish fathers down the path to a healthy style of fatherhood. Unlike the pedophile and the deadbeat, obviously, and unlike the thundergod and architect, the fool truly cares about his children—cares, even if only implicitly, about their liberation. He doesn't want to abuse. He doesn't want to abandon. He doesn't want to pontificate from on high. He doesn't want to stand back and observe his created objects. He wants to be involved, to insert himself into the lived reality of his children. However, usually because of some kind of inherent flaw, he comes across as a simpleton.

Michael Kimmel argues that the father as fool began to emerge in the early part of the 20th century. He writes, "Mocking fatherly incompetence became something of a boom industry in the popular press of the 1920s and 1930s, as in new comic strips like *Blondie* and plays like Clarence Day's *Life with Father*" (Kimmel, 1996, p. 205).

This construction of the father as fool follows on a period of extraordinary changes in the fatherly role in American culture, changes rooted in the birth of the country itself. As Kimmel tells the tale, America originally began to construct its own story as that of the rebellious son—the colonies—fighting against and overthrowing the tyrannical yoke of the father—England (Kimmel, 1996, p. 58). At the time of the revolution and prior to industrialization, a number of fatherly metaphors emerged in the American cultural narrative, coincident with, if not caused by, the patterns of American life itself (Kimmel, 1996, pp. 382–383). The "genteel father"—part of the agricultural tradition of the South, in particular—was marked by "easygoing sensuousness and elegance," dedicated to helping his children develop both masculine and feminine dimensions. The "evangelical father," constructed following the Second Great Awakening—the evangelical religious movement that swept America in the first third of the nineteenth century—was an authoritarian figure, particularly among the rural working class. The evangelical father was determined to discipline his children because they were, as sons and daughters of Adam and Eve, "inherently evil." The "moderate father," a metaphor present among urban merchants and entrepreneurs, was dedicated to shaping his children's characters, especially his sons'. He wanted to provide his sons with the "widest latitude for individual development." As America industrialized and urbanized itself, the moderate father became the dominant model, eclipsing the others.

At the same time, another phenomenon began to take shape, as Kimmel reminds us. Men and thus fathers "were increasingly exiled from the home … and so American fathers were increasingly estranged from the lives of their children, just as the workplace demanded an increasing amount of time and energy" (Kimmel, 1996, p. 58). As a result, mothers became the primary parental force in children's lives: the cult of motherhood began to emerge just as the father was becoming, in the terms of Karl Marx, a slave to the industrial wage system. We also see the separation of genders into public and private spheres: women and mothers became associated with the private domain of the home; men and fathers, with the public domain of work. Kimmel argues that the home became feminized and that men could not return to it "without fear of feminization" (Kimmel, 1996, p. 58). What is important to know for now is that men and fathers, because of economic changes in the social order, lost their places as fathers, whether genteel, evangelical or moderate. The moderate role won because, as Kimmel argues, it was the most amenable to the economic reality. If fathers can't guide or direct—activities that are central to the genteel and the evangelical father—they can allow their children to take charge of their own lives. The moderate father places the "greatest amount of moral responsibility ... upon the children" (Kimmel, 1996, pp. 382–383). Thus, by the time *Blondie* emerged in the 1920s and '30s, fathers were fools. They did not guide; they did not direct; they simply slept and ate and let their children be raised by the mothers or fend for themselves.

Kimmel reminds us that *Blondie* did not have the last word. As North Americans settled into a relatively calm period following both World War II and the Korean war, and before the revolutions of the late 1950s and 1960s, the cultural narrative fought against the image of father as fool (Kimmel, 1996, pp. 245–248). In 1954, *Life* magazine declared that year to be "the year of 'the domestication of the American man,' the climax of a decade dedicated to fatherhood and husbandry." Television shows such as *Father Knows Best, Ozzie and Harriet, Leave It to Beaver* and *The Donna Reed Show* constructed images of fathers who were anything but fools. They were domesticated, a full part of the private realm, always ready and willing to "listen to their children's problems, to help with homework, or to ferry them around their suburban neighborhoods" (Kimmel,

1996, pp. 247–248). At the same time, these fathers were shown to be relatively jobless: while they worked, work was "unimportant in the overall depiction of their lives." These fathers, in some ways, were actually mothers, at least as we have come to understand that term as used in suburban North America. Family life centred on the father and what the father was able to enact, through nurturance, for the family. Kimmel points to the 1950s as an era of television in which fathers were depicted as "nurturing, caring, and devoted to their children." This was a short-lived phenomenon: by the 1960s, many television fathers were either childless or buffoons (Kimmel, 1996, pp. 247–248). The classic film *Rebel Without a Cause* provides cinematic evidence of this fact: Jim (James Dean's character)'s father is a fool who wears an apron.[10]

This metaphor has shown no sign of disappearing. *Blondie* is still in syndication and Dagwood is still a fool: he sleeps and eats as the family continues to live around him. The North American cultural narrative's critique of father as fool is not located solely in pre–World War II America. Father as fool is firmly established in post–World War II America as well, and it continues to be updated.

Generally speaking, we see the father as fool in both the public and the private spheres. When the father attempts to become the nurturer, to become a proxy for the loving care of the mother, he is revealed as a fool. This is not surprising, given the split between parental roles, gender, and the public and the private. Women (and, thus, mothers) have come to be associated with the private sphere of life in the home. Men (and, thus, fathers) have come to be associated with the public sphere of life outside the home. Given this bifurcation, it is not surprising that the cultural narrative depicts fathers as fools when they try to enter the sphere of the woman and mother.

What is surprising is that the North American cultural narrative also shows the father to be a fool in the public sphere. This is the sphere where fathers, as men, are expected to excel, to be competent, expert, even heroic. While this is true of some, the cultural narrative shows many fathers to be relatively incompetent, inexpert, not heroic.

The contemporary tales that depict fathers as fools are commonly found in syndicated comic strips and children's picture books. Of course, they are part of the television universe as well: consider Homer Simpson, for example. Two examples are *FoxTrot*, a syndicated comic strip by Bill Amend, and the Berenstain Bears series of children's picture books by Jan and Stan Berenstain. Each offers a striking vantage point from which to see and understand the North American cultural narrative's creation and depiction of father as fool. Each has vast readerships across educational and class divides. *FoxTrot* shows us how father as fool is presented to a general newspaper readership—presumably early adolescents, adolescents and adults. The Berenstain Bears books, written for young children who are read to by older siblings and parents, and for beginning readers, show us how father as fool is presented to young children. This metaphor spans ages, audiences and media.

The Public Fool

FoxTrot depicts the Foxes, a suburban family of five. Mr. and Mrs. Fox—Roger and Andy—head the household, which also includes three school-age children: Peter, Paige and Jason. Andy, a newspaper columnist, works from home. Roger is a corporate flunky: he works in some type of non-descript job for some type of nondescript corporation for a boss who is a bit tyrannical.[11]

Roger's position as a worker follows the pattern set by Dagwood Bumstead in *Blondie*. Roger's position also manifests what Karl Marx depicts as wage slavery. Fathers who aren't bosses have no power in the workplace, or public sphere. As Karl Marx wrote in the *Communist Manifesto*, this was one of the consequences of capitalist industrialization. As the feudal order began to disintegrate with the rise of the capitalist industrial order, men and fathers were removed from their homes in order to make a living. Agricultural society began to collapse and families moved to urban areas to find work. Men and fathers began to leave home for hours and hours on end to labour in factories, selling the only thing they had: their ability to perform a task. They worked under conditions that were less than liberating, trading the oppressiveness of the feudal order for the oppressiveness of the industrial order. Feudal serfs became industrial workers. Instead of being slaves to their landed masters, they were now slaves to the industrial work order.

Roger Fox does not labour in a factory. He is a white-collar worker: he wears a tie and works in an office. Still, as a fool, he is not a satisfied or happy worker, contributing mightily to some great cause. Rather, he labours for a boss who mistreats him for ends that he himself has not constructed and does not understand or agree with. He works because he has to, indenturing himself to a system in which he is abused, in which he finds himself to be a fool.

In one *FoxTrot* strip, Roger Fox is called to the office of his boss, Mr. Pembrook (Amend, 1994, pp. 29–30). Roger, in typical fashion, stands with a pot-belly and crumpled tie, acting with subservient obedience. The initial frame of this series shows Roger as a fool. He is the poster boy for the suburban middle-age corporate worker: bald, overweight, badly dressed. Roger's series of facial expressions only furthers this image. His shocked, open-mouthed expression in the third frame provides comic relief, all the while making his plight clear: he is powerless. He needs his job in order to help feed, clothe, house and educate his family and he knows it.

Mr. Pembrook quickly establishes the power differential between himself and Roger when he calls his employee "Fox" rather than the informal and intimate "Roger" or the formal and polite "Mr. Fox." Roger, in turn, calls Mr. Pembrook "Sir," thus establishing the hierarchical nature of their relationship. Mr. Pembrook is in charge and Roger is not. Mr. Pembrook wants an enormous raise and wants Roger to compose a plan that justifies the request.

In the strips that follow, Roger is appalled, angry, rebellious and ultimately acquiescent. Mr. Pembrook's request for a raise comes at a time when the company is having financial trouble; many employees have been fired in order to cut costs. But Roger does not express his disgust and anger to Mr. Pembrook directly; he saves it for home.

When Roger returns to the relative safety of the private sphere, the home, he is able to express his anger. Andy, his wife, calmly asks whether he had a rough day at the office. Why? Because Roger is driving golf balls with great force into the living room wall. Golf is one of Roger's passions; here he uses it to emote. He is stunned by Mr. Pembrook's desire for a $300,000 raise, as we learn in the next strip, and stunned even more by the fact that he, Roger, must compose a presentation to justify the request.

There is hope that Roger will not play the fool to Mr. Pembrook's dictatorial scheme.

We see Roger, in the first three frames of the next strip, apparently talking to Mr. Pembrook. He is still deferential and courteous, referring to his boss as "sir" and apologizing for interrupting him and his busy schedule. He also strongly protests Mr. Pembrook's scheme: Roger argues that it is wrong for Mr. Pembrook to request the raise while his company is floundering and employees have lost their jobs. The last frame, however, delivers the punch line, showing Roger still to be a fool. We see that he is practising his speech to Mr. Pembrook in front of a dresser mirror, with his wife coaching him. Andy has apparently written the speech, providing Roger with a final Shakespearean line that Roger can't remember: the request for a raise is "Criminal, sir. Nay, heinous." Roger, admirably, is practising his rebellion, but one has to wonder who is the true rebel of the couple.

The final strip of the series answers this question. Andy delivers the speech in the form of questions, forcefully presenting an argument why Mr. Pembrook is wrong to ask for the raise and even daring to suggest that the CEO ask for a reduction in salary as a way to help return the company to profitability. Roger can only answer "no" to her cogent and powerful series of questions: "Did you tell him …?" As he does so, he reveals that he didn't rebel against the boss. As a result he is diminished as a worker, as a husband, as a man, as a father. The cartoonist represents this by showing Roger shrink under the onslaught of Andy's questions. By the third frame, with the final "no," Roger is tiny and cowed. He can't look Andy in the eye and his bottom jaw is thrust forward so that he can chew on his upper lip. The strip ends with Andy looking carefully at her husband; eyes squinted, she returns to the word "fine," which Roger used to describe the meeting with Mr. Pembrook. It becomes obvious that the meeting was "fine" only because Roger did not rebel. Instead, Roger went along with Mr. Pembrook in order to save his own job, and complimented his boss on his new tie. Rather than emerging as a liberating force, a hero on behalf of oppressed employees, on behalf of laid-off workers, on behalf of his wife, on behalf of his children, Roger solidified his status as bumpkin, as fool. In a reversal of gender roles, Roger is depicted as an emasculated weakling. Andy is the stronger of the two, the "man." She presses for rebellion against the corporate desiccation of human life. Roger simply bows and kowtows, doing his master's bidding.

Unfortunately for Roger, his foolishness extends beyond his work life. Even as the focus of his energy shifts back to his family, Roger is clueless, a true buffoon. The title of one of the collections of *FoxTrot* strips points to this foolishness: *Come Closer, Roger, There's a Mosquito on Your Nose*. The title refers to Andy's desire to whack Roger on the nose with a flyswatter when she and the children are irritated past comfort by mosquitoes while on a family camping expedition. Andy's face on the cover is one of pure anger and malice. Roger looks at her uncomprehendingly, holding a fishing pole. In the background, Peter, Paige and Jason are running away from the bugs and swatting them simultaneously. How did they end up camping? It was Roger's doing, of course.

The series of strips from which the collection's title comes perfectly exemplifies Roger's status as fool par excellence (Amend, 1997, pp. 48). If it is the man's and thus the father's role to negotiate the outdoors for his family, to mediate the relationship between nature and domestic life, to be an avatar of nature, Roger fails miserably.

Roger loves camping, loves the wilderness, loves to experience nature. No one else in his family does. Roger insists that they go. He has made reservation at Skeeter Falls, an eight-hour drive from where the family lives. The Foxes arrive only to find their own "personal ranger" waiting for them.

Roger is excited, enlivened, happy: he is the opposite of his work self. His eyes are fresh, his eyebrows jaunty as he tells Andy how great Skeeter Falls is. What he misses is the ranger's netting, setting up the final joke of this strip. As the ranger stands in front of him, ready for bug season, as mosquitoes swarm around his own head, Roger finally asks the obvious question: "So where does the name 'Skeeter Falls' come from?"

In the next strip, the Ranger tells Roger, now busy swatting and scratching, that "The waterfalls, now they peak usually sometime in May when all the mountain snow is melting. But the *skeeters*, this is *their* peak time of year. No spot on earth has more mosquitoes per acre than we do in August." The Ranger then turns to Roger and says, "I am praying that you knew that." Roger only turns to yell to Andy, "Honey, did we pack any insect repellent?" Roger himself didn't, just as he didn't know that he had led his family into an earthly mosquito-infested hell.

The ever-popular Berenstain Bears books, first published in 1962 and read by parents to their children, by early childhood educators to their students, and by children themselves, tell the story of Papa Bear, Mama Bear, Brother Bear and Sister Bear as they live their lives in Bear Country. Typically, these books present human life in the guise of animal life, a standard strategy in literature written for children. Typically, these books present the father as fool. Like Roger Fox, Father Bear is a buffoon. His interactions with his family serve comedy, not liberation: he is incapable of guiding his children to anything because he is pompous, blind and often a child himself.

One of the earliest Berenstain Bears books appears as part of Dr. Seuss' I Can Read It All By Myself series of Beginner Books. Titled *The Bears' Vacation*, it depicts a father bear, a mother bear and "small bear" on vacation at a beachfront cottage. (These characters have not yet taken on what will become their classic names.)

The story, written in the ABCB rhyme pattern typical of Dr. Seuss books, involves the father bear teaching his son the rules of safety to be followed at the beach. The story opens with the mother bear admonishing the small bear to stay near her, even as he is running to jump into the ocean. The mother bear emerges as the typical mom: she wants to keep her child in sight to be sure he is safe. She wants to keep him close to home: the orbit of the domestic sphere, the sphere she controls.

On the very next page, however, the father bear pompously dismisses the mother bear's concerns. With an imperial wave of his hand, he tells the mother bear, "Don't you worry./Don't you fear./I'll show him/all the dangers here" (Berenstains, 1968, p. 9). He thus moves small bear into a world where the private and public meet, and provides the set-up for the series of ironic mishaps to follow. The mother should worry and should have fear. Like Roger Fox, Father Bear will show he is not capable of protecting his child when he moves with that child into the larger world. Father Bear does show small bear all the dangers of the beach, but in the process endangers both their lives.

For instance, Father Bear immediately tells his son, "Then here is the first rule/you should know./Obey all warning signs!/Look around./Are there any warning signs/to be found?" (11). As he asks this question, the father bear tosses his towel over such a sign. We discover, with small bear, that the sign warns of a strong undertow. Father Bear, imperilling his own safety, has already jumped into the water. Small bear yells to his father that he has found the warning sign. We then see small bear rescuing his father, who is now in danger of drowning. Small bear, after rescuing his father and seeing him half-drowned and exhausted, has learned well: it is dangerous to swim in areas where there is an undertow. We, as readers, laugh at the father: what a fool!

The remainder of the book is one calamity after another. The father bear teaches through demonstration. He dives onto a log after warning small bear to be careful when diving. He crashes himself and small bear into rocks while surfing, after having warned small bear to "beware of all rocks/ when surfing at sea" (24). He is attacked by large turtles after warning small bear to be careful when touching things. And so it goes. The father bear becomes the clownish teacher: small bear learns by watching the comedy unfold.

The book ends with small bear rescuing himself and his father from an oncoming ocean liner while they are sailing, taking control of the boat and steering it out of the way of the ship. In the final illustration, we see small bear sailing the boat upside down, with his father tied to the mast, looking bruised and dazed. The mother bear stands on the deck of their cottage, looking worried. Small bear cheerfully announces, while heroically sailing the boat and his father back to safety, "Ma!/You don't have to worry/any more!/Pa taught me how/to be safe at the shore!" (62–63).

The Private Fool

Not only are Roger Fox and Papa Bear incompetent fools in public, the realm where men, in the industrial and post-industrial order, are meant to excel, they are fools even at home. In fact, because we are able to see a direct comparison between them and their wives, they look even more foolish at home than they do in public. The mothers in these tales are shown to be wise, competent, caring homemakers. The fathers, in contrast, are bumpkins when they become directly involved in the lives of their families at home.

One memorable series of *FoxTrot* strips, anthologized in *Welcome to Jasorassic Park* (Amend, 1998, pp. 104–108), explores Roger's inability to stand in for Andy while she is away at a newspaper convention.

The first strip in the series shows Jason in the third panel, fantasizing: "Oh, man. I can just picture it now—wild, unrestrained, out-of-control lunacy."

Peter asks, "At the convention?"

Jason replies, "No, no. Here with Dad in charge."

Peter ends the strip by saying, "By the way, Mom wants us to memorize this fire escape plan."

The comedy is subtle, cutting and at Roger's expense. As far as Jason is concerned, placing Dad in charge of the household is inviting chaos. Peter doesn't disagree. In fact, Jason's observation allows Peter to segue into a request made by Mom: memorize the fire escape routes. Why? Because having Dad in charge necessitates knowing how to exit the house quickly in case of emergency.

Andy, preparing for her time away, is fulfilling the role of supermom here. She is leaving the family for a few days, but she can't leave her husband and children to their own devices. She has made meals for them in advance, ready to remove from the freezer and heat. She also feels the need to remind Roger to take out the trash.

Roger, stunned by Andy's lack of trust in his ability to care for the home, their children and even himself, asks in frustration, "How pathetically helpless do you think I am?" His eyes are raised, his hands spread out, both indicating his level of incredulity. The next frame simply presents Andy looking at Roger without speaking, as if the answer to the question is obvious. She refuses to answer, however, moving on to the next item on her list: she has given a neighbour a key to the house in case Roger or the kids lock themselves out. Roger ends the strip with a bit of anger: his eyes are intense, his mouth narrow and turned downward.

The subsequent strips in the series demonstrate that Roger is simply not capable of acting in a way that helps his children discover liberation: he is barely able to keep them safe, to feed them, to care for their needs. In one, Jason asks his father whether the family can order pizza for dinner. Roger replies, "If I order pizza, it's like throwing in the towel. No sir. I'm cooking us real, stove-top dinners, even if it kills me." The next frame shows Roger being incinerated by flames exploding from a frying pan. The strip ends with Roger collapsed on the floor. We see only his right arm and hand stretching up from the bottom, holding out money for Peter to buy pizza.

In another strip, Roger valiantly tries to wash the family's dirty clothes. The result: the clothes shrink to doll-size proportions and the colours run.

Papa Bear fully demonstrates his private incompetence in the book *Life with Papa*, which is full of gender tension, centred around the relative domestic value of the male and the female, of the father and the mother. *Life with Papa*, interestingly, was distributed by "McDonald's in cooperation with the American Library Association." A restaurant that caters to children joined with librarians nationwide to promote reading: a laudable goal. One wonders, in the case of *Life with Papa*, whether they also intended to promote the image of father as fool.

The narrative arc of *Life with Papa* is simple. A cousin of Mama Bear's is on the verge of delivering a baby, and Mama Bear wonders whether she could go to help her, since "being a first time mama bear isn't easy." Papa Bear, helpfully, encourages her to do so: "Sounds like a good idea to me … What's to stop you?" Mama Bear takes umbrage at this, asserting her role as the mistress of the house. She claims that many things would stop her: "The cooking, the cleaning, the shopping and all the other things that need tending to?" Papa Bear, "puffing out his chest," declares that he will do it, and do it better than Mama: "Not only can I handle the job, but I can handle it half-asleep with one hand tied behind me." This nearly leads to a fight between Mama Bear and Papa Bear, reminiscent of the famous gender tension between Annie Oakley and Frank Butler in the musical *Annie Get Your Gun*: "Anything you can do, I can do better."

The battle is interrupted when Mama receives a call. Her cousin has delivered twins! Mama immediately decides to go help for a few days, leaving Papa in charge. She says, "I'll do what I can before I leave and just hope for the best."

Clearly, she doesn't think that Papa is up to the task. Papa disagrees, yelling to her as she leaves, "I can handle things here at home! No trouble at all!" Famous last words.

The story proceeds to demonstrate Papa Bear's complete and total incompetence. His first act once he is in charge? To beat the rugs: he wants to given them a "good cleaning" in "the old-fashioned way." He proceeds to beat them outside on the line, but does so right next to the laundry that Mama Bear has left out to dry. Now the rugs are clean but the clothes are filthy. Papa Bear is not worried when the cubs point this out to him. He tells them, "It'll surely rain before Mama comes back and rinse it all off."

What happens next only confirms Mama's opinion. Much to the cubs' chagrin, Papa Bear then makes them lunch: his famous "triple-flip honey-mustard pancakes." They are less than excited by the thought, especially when they realize that they will have to eat pancakes that have been scraped off the ceiling: Papa Bear was a little too wild with his flips. After lunch he makes a fire, but fails to open the flue. As a result, smoke fills the Bears' house. Papa Bear tries to extinguish the fire with a feather pillow, which promptly breaks, sending feathers everywhere. It takes Brother and Sister Bear to put out the fire, sensibly using water.

Fortunately for Papa Bear, his neighbour, Mr. Skunk, sees the smoke and feathers "billowing from the tree house windows" and comes to help. He organizes all the forest creatures to help clean the house: "Birds and butterflies fanned the smoke," "Squirrels dusted with their tails," "Frogs snagged feathers with their sticky tongues," and "Raccoons rinsed the dirty wash in the brook."

All this work was accomplished just in time for Mama's return. Her cousin hadn't needed her help after all and she came back later that same day. Papa Bear had managed to bring ruin to his house in less than 10 hours and was saved only by good friends. Mama Bear doesn't know what happened and even remarks, "The house looks wonderful, my dear ... However did you manage it?" Papa Bear chooses not to speak honestly: "Well ... it did take a little doing," assuming responsibility for the clean house. Only the cubs are voices of honesty, but to themselves alone: "and ... a little *un*doing."

If real fathers are meant to look to characters like Papa Bear and Roger Fox for inspiration, they don't have much hope. Granted, these two characters aren't deadbeats, thundergods or architects, but they are fools, through and through. To what metaphor, then, do fathers turn? Many men who choose to have a close connection with their children choose the metaphor Mr. Mom.

6

Mr. Mom

"Here is Sophie's mommy."

—15-month-old

"I am Mr. Mom today."

—College professor

Images

1

The doorbell rang. Standing outside was my son's friend and a tall, large man—presumably the boy's father. The father was dressed in work clothes: jeans, leather boots sporting steel-cap toes, flannel shirt, baseball-style cap with a company name on it. I opened the door and he greeted me heartily. I invited him in. As his son and mine went off to play, this dad stayed for a while, eager to chat, enjoying a new connection.

Images
2

We used to call him "Superdad." My wife and I, sometimes by ourselves and sometimes with another couple, would sit in the park next to the Bixler playlot in Hyde Park, deep in the Southside of Chicago, and watch the children play. We were graduate students all: happy but longing, some day, for children. One family always caught our eye. Dad and daughter and son. Most parents, save those of toddlers, sat on benches watching their children play. Not Superdad. He was play itself. Up the poles, down the slides. Across the monkey bars, through the tunnels. He and his children laughed, ran, scooted, slid, climbed, laughed, and did it all again and again.

Both these men might be labelled with the name *Mr. Mom*, a term that achieved cinematic stardom in the 1983 film *Mr. Mom*, starring Michael Keaton and Teri Garr as Jack and Caroline Butler. In general, "Mr. Mom" refers to fathers who have taken on the role of the stay-at-home mother. Who hasn't seen fathers taking on elements of the motherly role: toting babies in carseats, backpacks, front carriers? Who hasn't seen fathers escorting children to play dates, daycare centres, schools? At the same time, who hasn't seen fathers who are more wedded to their work than to their spouse? More concerned about giving birth to and nurturing their professional lives or hunting or sports than nurturing their own children?

Play Dates, Birthday Parties and Parks

The play date is a contemporary phenomenon brought about by at least two factors: the geographical spread of families within a single school district, and the construction of loose-knit neighbourhoods. Schools in rural suburbia, as I refer to my town, draw from housing clusters that are up to 15 minutes apart by car. They are not connected by sidewalks and often are separated by major roads. While these housing clusters are supposedly neighborhoods—often given names in order to mark them as a unit—they are not neighbourhoods, really. They are too vast and thus too unconnected to be anything other than a collection of houses marketed by enterprising developers as communities.

My family, like many others, lives in a school district that draws students from a large radius of our town. When my son started first grade, he began to make friends from all over this geographic area. These friends were all in his classroom, speaking to the power of local community: he identified with them and befriended them. Yet none of them lived in our neighbourhood. So, he had play dates: we would call the parents of a friend from school and ask whether the boy could come over to play. My wife and I were always interested to see which parent would bring the child. Usually, it was the mother. However, one friend was almost always brought over by his father: the dad of the first image, above.

I came to see this dad often over the next few years. He was deeply committed to his son's and daughter's lives. He took them to play dates, to birthday parties, to all sorts of places that were, in the main, dominated by mothers. His commitment to his children's lives, demonstrated by his happy willingness to tote them around to friends' houses and parties, belied his masculine image. Despite the fact that he worked outside the home and was unfamiliar with feminist theory and literature, he became part of the female world of play dates and parties.

"Superdad," in the second image above, had also shifted into a new reality. First, he, not his wife, brought the children to the park. For the most part, it was the mothers who toted the children to Bixler playlot, even in Hyde Park, Chicago, which has more than its share of feminist men, of married couples with different last names. Second, he did not sit and chat with the other parents: he played with abandon, entering into the fantastic and most likely phantasmal world that his children inhabited. One could suggest that he entered into play because his only other choice was to sit alone. My own experience and observation have taught me that mothers are not always welcoming to fathers at parks, even when the father has attempted, however awkwardly, to bridge the silent strangeness and talk. On the other hand, I have seen mothers strike up an acquaintance with other mothers very quickly.

My experience is corroborated by that of Andrea Doucet's husband, Derek. In her book *Do Men Mother?* Doucet relates her husband's experience of taking their daughter to a "moms and tots" playgroup in Cambridge, England. As she writes, "My husband was assured that *moms* was a generic term for parents ... yet the welcome he received was a cold one at best" (Doucet, 2006, p. 10). My own experience and that of Doucet's husband remind us that it is no easy task for fathers to move into a new space in which they nurture, care for, attend to their children. Even if they embrace their role as "Mr. Mom," mothers—here I mean the parent who not only nurtures but is also biologically a female—do not necessarily or easily embrace these men as "Mr. Mom." As Doucet notes, her husband's attempt "to blend in was a harsh reminder that gender does matter, at least in some community sites, when it comes to just *who* is doing the mothering" (Doucet, 2006, pp. 10–11). One might think that "community sites" like Hyde Park, Chicago, and Cambridge, England—filled with academics, artists, feminists—would lend themselves to so-called progressive gender relationships whereby men and women nurture and welcome each other into nurturing communities. This, Doucet points out, is not always the case.

However, Superdad was there to play. How do I know this? The look on his face, the intensity of his actions, and his pleasure-filled laugh all demonstrated his desire not to watch his children, not to chat with the other adults, but to play—to enter into the world of climbing, sliding, running, jumping, swinging—that children easily and delightfully inhabit. Superdad could have brought a book or a computer to occupy his energy and time, as another father I know used to do: his children were old enough to play alone. But he didn't. He played.

◎   ◎   ◎

The Search for a New Identity

Even as many men struggle to find a new identity for themselves amid the ruins of postmodernity, they find that no one metaphor has arisen to replace the fallen ones. Clearly, the liberating father won't choose to be a pedophile, a deadbeat, a thundergod, an architect and will hope to avoid being a fool. Fatherhood movements are attempting to name new metaphors, some of which are simply variants on traditional father metaphors, albeit with a kinder and gentler twist.[12] Terms such as disciplinarian, breadwinner, and "self-sacrificing protector" are part of this movement (Gavanas, 2002, p. 230).

In addition, feminists are often skeptical of the ways in which men are trying to redefine themselves as fathers. Attempts to redefine fatherhood are problematic, at least from certain feminist perspectives. As R. W. Connell (1995) suggests in *Masculinities*, feminists such as Barbara Ehrenreich wonder if men are really committed to creating a new and more just society. These feminists think that men want the benefits that come from feminism—for example, the ability to reconceive fatherhood in ways that allow them to nurture—without giving up the privilege of power that comes from being a man (Connell, 1995, p. 42). In short, the "new sensitive man" (Connell, 1995, p. 42) wants to have his cake and eat it, too.

Within this mess of unacceptable metaphors, another, which is present throughout the North American cultural narrative, genuinely attends to fathers who condemn pedophiles and deadbeats, who no longer ascribe to being Zeus or The Lord, who refuse to walk away from their offspring like an architect who designs the product and leaves it for others to fill, to shape, to care for. That metaphor is Mr. Mom.

As an academic, I am blessed to have a job with a relatively flexible schedule. I am also blessed to work on a college campus that has an excellent early childhood centre. In fact, one reason I left a tenure-track position at another college to come to my current school is this early childhood centre. My son was almost two when I was interviewing. When I saw the centre, I could easily imagine him there, part of my work world.

In short, I have taken my children to work with me. This has allowed me to visit their classrooms daily, to eat lunch with them and read them stories after their lunch as they settle in for rest time, to meet their mates, to establish relationships with their teachers, and to play basketball and soccer with them and their friends in the afternoons when I come to take them home. Thus, in a strange twist of postmodern reality, I see my children between the hours of 7 a.m. and 3 p.m. more than my wife does. As a middle school guidance counsellor, she leaves the house at 7 a.m. and returns at around 3:30 or 4:00 p.m.

One morning, when my daughter, Sophie, was almost two years old, I made breakfast for her and her brother and packed their lunches. I played with them and then loaded them into the car. I dropped my son at his elementary school, then my daughter and I continued on to my campus and the early childhood centre. When we arrived, we walked into the centre, greeting staff, faculty and many parents, all of whom, like me, were bringing their children to school, and many of whom, like me, are fathers rather than mothers.

I took my daughter to her classroom, designed for the youngest children in the centre. We opened the sliding gate, walked in, and closed the gate behind us, lest some adventurous toddler escape into the bigger world. My daughter and I removed her coat and placed it and her lunch box in her "cubby." Just as I was turning to greet one of the teachers, one of my daughter's classmates called out excitedly, "Here is Sophie's mommy!"

"Sophie's mommy?"

"Sophie's mommy?"

Did this child who called me a mom know anything about theories of gender identity? Of course not. Did she intend to insult me? No. Did she intend to praise me? I don't think so. She was simply naming the presence of a being, much like she might point to that creature we call a bird and say, "bird." This child was beginning to name, and she used the name available to her: mommy. I was, simply put, fulfilling a function that matched with what in her head was the function of the mother. Who brings the child to school? Mommy. Who helps the child take off her coat? Mommy. Who helps the child put her coat and lunch into her cubby? Mommy. Who talks to and plays with the other children when she has time? Mommy. For this child, mothering was totally distinct from gender. Chromosomes, secondary sex characteristics, the presence or absence of a womb, types of clothing—none of these had anything to do with mothering. What defined mothering was not gender identity or gender markings but function. As the female dragon Kazul says to her princess, Cimorene, in *Talking to Dragons*, the first book of Jane Yolen's feminist Enchanted Forest Chronicles, being the king of dragons has nothing to do with gender. Female dragons can be king. The office is a matter of function, not of gender.

Significantly, my daughter's classmate's metaphor for me indicates the ruins in which fathers now operate. Rejecting the metaphors of pedophile, deadbeat, thundergod, architect and fool, I had gladly stepped into a new world in which I was not, and am not, the thunderous figure promised by the threat "Wait till your father gets home." I had gladly stepped into a new world in which I was not, and am not, the absent architect, the father who disappeared literally or figuratively from his children's lives. I was and am present. I make their breakfasts; I make their lunches; I take them to school, wipe their noses, comfort them, cajole them, love them. To that little girl in my daughter's classroom, I am a mom.

My mother-in-law has never called me a mom. Unlike my daughter's little classmate, she understands the link between gender and function: those humans we call female serve as mothers; those beings we call male serve as fathers. With this gender identity comes a function not at all unlike the function assigned to mothers by my daughter's classmate. My mother-in-law has long thought like that little girl: mothers are more present in the lives of their children than fathers are. Fathers, for her, disappear: they are architects.

My mother-in-law called our house one morning. The children were both off from school. My wife had to go to work for a meeting, so I arranged my schedule in order to be at home with them. When I answered the phone, my mother-in-law expressed surprise.

"Are you babysitting the children today?" she asked.

My presence at home did not match the function she had assigned to the position of father. It was I, not my wife, who was supposed to go away during the day. It was I who was to be outside the home when the children were at home. She could make sense of my presence only by invoking the metaphor of babysitting. In her experience, fathers did not stay at home with the children while the mothers went to work.

Moreover, the metaphor *babysitter* is implicitly and inevitably gender specific. While it might not *denote* female, it most certainly *connotes* female. Aware of the gender identification assigned to mothers and fathers, my mother-in-law could not ask, "Are you mothering the children today?" As awkward as that phrase might be, it would capture what I was doing: caring for and nurturing my children. Mothering, as Larry May argues, "in common parlance … refers exclusively to acts of nurturance and caretaking" (May, 1998, p. 30). Syntactic awkwardness aside, my mother-in-law could not have asked whether I was mothering her grandchildren because that would have not made sense in her world view. Mothers "mother." Fathers … well, what do fathers do when they are alone at home with their children? She moved to the next best metaphor: babysitter. I was fulfilling a female function, in her eyes, and she needed somehow to name it.

My mother-in-law could not ask whether I was "fathering" the children today, even if our syntax allowed for such a strange phrase. She could not do this, as May might agree, because usually when we talk of "fathering" a child we usually refer to the act of procreating. As May says, this is sign of how low our expectations for fathers are: "'fathering' can refer merely to the acts of insemination and impregnation" (May, 1998, p. 30). In this understanding, my mother-in-law would have been asking a very personal and private question: in any case, I could not be "fathering" the children since they were already born.

As Theodore Cohen has argued, "For much of the 20th century, Americans have associated fathers with the act of working and the responsibility of 'providing' for their families. This image of fathers arises more from general assumptions about men and the dominant ideologies of gender than from any empirical evidence" (Cohen, 1993, p. 1). My mother-in-law knows that my wife and I live in a way that challenges the idea that fathers are limited to procreation and provision. Thus, she herself has "empirical evidence" that, at least in the case of her daughter and son-in-law, another metaphor is in play. However, her world view, like that of most of us, has been informed by a particular symbol: the symbol of father as provider. Townsend's study suggests, however, that men "consider being involved in child care and child rearing as a choice (to be 'involved'), but women do not" (Townsend, 2002, pp. 81–82). This means, perhaps that it is "natural" for women to nurture, but it is not "natural" for men to nurture. (I have placed *natural* in quotation marks to call this term into question. *Natural* here could mean that our cultural codes—our symbols—have led us to think in one way. Other ways are possible: we can discover new symbols that will inform us in different ways.)

When an action provides empirical evidence to counter the symbol that has informed her, my mother-in-law doesn't know how to change the symbol. Thus, she moves to another symbol to help explain the change. This demonstrates that symbols—here, metaphors—do indeed shape our world views, our understanding of how the world works. It also shows how difficult it is to develop new metaphors that better speak to the reality of human life.

Strangely, and this is the nature of metaphor, *babysitter* has ramifications other than the obvious. While it suggested that I was a female, it also suggested that I was caring for my children either as an act of wage labour or as a favour. Babysitters work for money: they exchange their labour for a wage. Neighbours or friends babysit as a favour. They won't accept cash payment for caring for the children of others. Instead, they become involved in a complex gift economy. For instance, my wife and I would on occasion ask our next-door neighbour to babysit our younger child. Did we pay her? No: she would have been insulted had we even offered payment. Did we give her gifts at appropriate times during the year? Of course. Did I help her husband move impossibly heavy furniture? Yes. This was all part of the gift economy.

Even fathers (or babysitters) refer to themselves as "Mr. Mom." Men who are present in their children's lives are moving into new territory and need a way to name themselves because there is no other name available. Consider, for instance, a colleague of mine. Once he called me on a Friday to tell me that he would not be working that day, since his children were sick. His own schedule for work was light, but his wife's was heavy: she had to go to work. The result? "I am Mr. Mom today."

Like my mother-in-law, he understands the gender dynamics surrounding fatherhood and motherhood. A present and caring father, he would never call himself a babysitter for his children. Highly aware of irony as a verbal technique, he would never say "I am mom, today." Rather, he places, as is the practice of commonplace culture, the male title *Mr.* with the female word *mom*. The result is a wonderful ironic play on gender and parental function. The gender connotations of *mom* are called into question by *Mr.* Can a mom be a mister? Simultaneously, the gender denotation of *Mr.* is called into question by *mom*. Can a mister be a mom?

Curious and troubling is my friend's use of the term. Why couldn't he simply say that he was at home with his sick children? Why did he need to qualify this act of fatherhood by calling himself "Mr. Mom"? Because the metaphors for father are falling apart. My colleague has committed himself to living a fatherhood of "presence": he wants to be involved in his children's lives, mundane and extraordinary as they can be. While fathers who are present in their children's lives find ways to do so that fulfill the function of mother, they have no name. Children don't know what to call them; mothers-in-law don't know what to call them; they don't know what to call themselves.

◎   ◎   ◎

Fathers as Mothers on the Edge of Time

Unfortunately, we don't have good options readily available in the North American cultural narrative. Yet if a man fulfills the functions of mothering, then it makes sense that he should be called a mother.

This term is historically reasonable because, as we noted earlier, coincident with the urbanization and industrialization of America was the split between the genders relative to public and private space. The home became feminized, dominated by women and mothers (Kimmel, 1996, p. 58).[13] and women and mothers became primarily responsible, at least in the North American cultural narrative if not in reality, for rearing children. When fathers raise, attend to and care for the children, fathers are acting as mothers. As Cohen argues, "Parenting was culturally perceived as 'mothering,' in that it implied nurturance, an activity seen as natural to women but foreign to men ... fathers' connections to their children were portrayed as chiefly financial; good fathers were 'good providers' and good providers made good fathers" (Cohen, 1993, p. 2).

The term *Mr. Mom* is attractive because it speaks to the liberating power of motherhood and mothering. When a soldier is dying on the battlefield, so the story goes, he will call for his mother. Questions of accuracy aside, this cliché points to the power of motherhood and mothering. The mother provides psychic sustenance to the dying soldier, helping him find deliverance in that horrible moment when he knows that he is bound by death.

The mother plays an equally important role in the psyche of those who are alive. Consider, for example, Mrs. Sowerby, Dickon's mother in Frances Hodgson Burnett's classic children's novel *The Secret Garden*. While Colin's father, Mr. Craven, is an absentee father, a deadbeat in the sense that he has all but abandoned his son, Mrs. Sowerby—a Yorkshire mother raising twelve children in a small cottage—is seen by all as the paragon of wisdom and virtue. In one sequence, she truly emerges as the earth mother: she provides sustenance for hungry children—Colin and Mary—who are becoming more fully human because of their work with, and their connection to, the land.

Mrs. Sowerby sends fresh milk and cottage buns for the children to eat as they garden. When her son Dickon first provides the food to them, near the novel's end, the narrator speaks for Colin and Mary: "What a wonderful thing for Mrs. Sowerby to think of! What a kind, clever woman she must be!" Then Colin adds, "Magic is in her just as it is in Dickon ... It makes her think of ways to do things—nice things. She is a Magic person" (Burnett, 1998, p. 267). For Colin, this is the highest praise. As a sickly child, shunned and feared by his own father and without a mother (she died in childbirth), Colin finds in "magic" (which is, in essence, the regenerative power of the earth) all he has not had in his life. Colin venerates Mrs. Sowerby because she is magic: the earth mother herself.

Given our cultural narrative's veneration of the mother, given the link between mothers and nurturing, mothers and nourishment, it makes sense that we would call the nurturing father "Mr. Mom." Moreover, Mr. Mom offers, as feminist theologians suggest is the case with our visions of God, a neat reversal: the historically oppressed and forgotten becomes that which names what Kenneth Burke, in his brilliant book, *The Rhetoric of Religion*, calls our "god terms" (Burke, 1961, p. 33). God terms are those words and phrases by which and with which we orient our lives. If mother is one of the most—if not the most—important images in the lives of our children, a god term by which children organize their lives, then fathers could do worse than to become, at least metaphorically, mothers.

The Septimus Heap series of fantasy novels written for children clearly reveals the power and place of mother. *Magyk*, the first book in the series, depicts the loss and rediscovery of the seventh son of a seventh son of a family of wizards. Septimus, the lost and rediscovered one, is kidnapped as an infant. An evil wizard, who had been deposed from his position of power and wishes to regain it, realizes that the child holds great magical promise, as seventh sons of seventh sons do. In a twist of fate, however, the evil wizard is given the wrong infant—an infant with no magical promise whatsoever. Septimus goes on to become a member of the Young Army and is given a number for a name: boy 412. It becomes clear that this boy 412 is more than a member of the Young Army, although he himself does not realize it. Readers are only given hints, of course. It is only at the end of the novel that his full ability becomes evident. And it is only at the very end of the novel that his identity becomes known to all. How so? His great-great-Aunt Zelda, a white witch, uses her magic to discover his parentage and family. Only when he asks who his mother is does it become fully clear that he is, indeed, the seventh son of the seventh son, the lost child now rediscovered: Septimus Heap.

Significantly, boy 412 did not ask who his father was, although his father loved his children dearly and had even given up the chance to become the ExtraOrdinary Wizard (the most powerful wizard) in order to be a father. He wanted to be able to read books to his children and put them to bed. Rather, boy 412 asks about his mother. This shows that lineage is rooted not in the loins of the father but in the womb of the mother, despite the practice of patriarchal societies in which women forgo the use of their own family name in order to take on the identity of the father's family, and in which the child is routinely given the father's family name rather than the mother's. As the earlier discussion of the problem of bastards showed, men can easily claim or not claim their child. Children are identified with the mother, not with the father. When boy 412 asks who his mother is so that he might know who he is, he simply does what most children seem to do: gravitate toward the mother in time of need, be it psychic or somatic. Mothers provide identity. Fathers do not.

Marge Piercy's *Woman on the Edge of Time*, a work of feminist utopian fiction, radically develops this metaphor. The novel involves the intersection of two worlds: the United States of the 1970s and the United States (or, more accurately, the geographic area once known as the United States) of hundreds of years in the future. The novel centres on a Latina, Connie, who lives a troubled life in the 1970s: her daughter has been removed from her care because she is an unfit mother, she has had a series of abusive relation-ships with men, and she is in and out of a mental hospital. While Connie is in the hospital, the people of the future make contact with her: they have developed the ability to travel through time and she is "receptive," having the ability to be contacted. At once, the intersection between dystopic present and utopic future begins: Connie is brought to the future and comes to know the future society intimately.

One aspect of that society that she learns about is par-enting. In the utopic future, the word *father* and the practice of "fathering" have been excised from the feminist, egalitar-ian culture. Instead, there are only mothers, but mothers particular and peculiar: men and women both are mothers and each child has three (Piercy, 1976, pp. 102–106, 116, 133–136). Moreover, women no longer carry embryos in their wombs: instead, embryos gestate in breeder houses full of artificial uteri, and men and women breastfeed. Women do so through their natural ability. Men are given injections of hormones to develop mammary capability, seemingly latent, hiding behind the nipples that have no apparent purpose on the male torso. Why does Piercy imagine a utopia in which "father" has disappeared, in which "mother" has become the dominant metaphor for parenting? When Connie learns of this type of parenting, she, serving as our representative, is horrified.

Luciente, one of the major characters from the imagined future who made contact with Connie, explains that women had to give up their final power, what Connie calls the power of blood and milk. If the culture was ever going to move beyond a devastating and dangerous patriarchy, then the fundamental power dynamics at the centre of all cultures—that power dynamic involving men and women and birth—had to be broken so that men could become nurturers, so that women could become more than nurturers. As Luciente and her culture see it, as long as men were able to be unconnected to birth and birthing, as long as women were given that sole power, the culture would careen dangerously out of control. Men would use the power that comes from being able to impregnate women and walk away from them and their children to control women and try to control other men. Women would use the power that comes from the womb to try to control men and other women. The original division of labour and power of production that is based in reproduction leads to schism and oppression. Once women had given up their primal power and shared it with men, the true revolution could begin: men and women alike could mother, could connect in fundamental ways with each other and their children.

Piercy's vision of fetuses in incubators, of a world in which both motherhood and fatherhood have disappeared in favour of genderless parenting, of a world of the breasted male, is far from reality, far from what even the most progressive people would like to see happen. Even if people wanted to see fathers move beyond what they are now, even if they were willing to diminish the power of the mother so that the father might be empowered, this doesn't mean that these same people would give up wombs, "natural" birth, female breasts and male chests.

The Problem with Mr. Mom

However sensible and attractive the metaphor of Mr. Mom is, the substitution of mother for father is triply problematic. First, fathers are metaphorized as female, raising a host of unresolved gender issues. Second, *mother* itself has multiple connotations. To say that father is mother, that dad is mom, leaves unanswered this question: What, precisely, is mom? Third, motherhood is made the standard of good parenthood, when another standard is in order.

To say that the father is Mr. Mom is to figure the male as female. While this has wonderful ironic power, it is problematic because it ignores a host of questions about gender identification. First among these is whether the facts of maleness and femaleness are meaningless. If fathers are mothers, and thus if men are women, is there nothing to male identity?

One extreme claims that maleness is entirely socially constructed, that it has no "natural" meaning: it has meaning only because particular communities give it meaning. This, so the argument roughly goes, accounts for the differences in maleness across time and space. For example, how else can we account for the phenomenon that men wearing white powdered wigs was considered masculine in one era and country but not in another? Or that highly muscled men were considered masculine in one era and country but not in another?

The other extreme claims that maleness is, in a fundamental sense, "natural." Men are men because of what nature has endowed them with: physical characteristics, such as broad shoulders and a penis; and psychological characteristics, driven by testosterone, perhaps, such as the willingness and desire to inflict physical punishments on opponents, whether on the battlefield or on the sports field. For example, something has to account for the lack of lineups in a men's public toilet and the extraordinarily long lineups in a women's public toilet. That something is the penis. A penis allows a male to urinate from a standing position, thus inalterably placing him and his sons in certain and unique arrangements, such as urinating on a tree in the woods, or in a urinal in a men's bathroom.

Both extremes of this conversation are correct. Neither side can sensibly exclude the other. Nor, as Connell (1995) argues, is some sort of compromise between the two sides in order. It is difficult to imagine that taking some points from one extreme and some points from another and melding them together can adequately deal with what Connell reminds us is the irreducible nature of the male body and, in addition, the complex ways in which we construct that male body with our symbols systems, such as clothing, words and hairstyles. There is a being that we call the male, a being that is constructed both by nature and by words and clothes and music and art. To simply say that the best metaphor for father is Mr. Mom is to ignore the complex gendered reality that is the father.

While this is not exactly the point Doucet makes in her own answer to the title question of her book—Do men mother?—her thoughts expand this conversation in helpful ways. Doucet herself wants to avoid two feminist extremes (Doucet, 2006, pp. 20–26). On one hand, some say that men do not and cannot mother: there is an irreducible difference between men and women, fathers and mothers. On the other hand, some argue that, indeed, men do mother: mothering is not necessarily linked to gender. Doucet instead wants "to chart a third path down the middle" (Doucet, 2006, p. 25).

One way she does so is to call into question the question itself. She argues that the question—Do men mother?—is problematic for a number of reasons, including this one: the question "implies that we are looking at fathering and fathers' experiences of emotional, community and moral responsibilities through a maternal lens" (Doucet, 2006, p. 222). Why is this a problem? For two reasons, Doucet argues. First, "other ways of nurturing are pushed into the shadows and obscured" (Doucet, 2006, p. 222). (I will discuss the issue of nurturing further in the next chapter: Dad Incarnate.) Second, the question is methodologically flawed, reversing what feminists have long claimed as a problem with the study of women's experience and history: men should not be submerged by women's terms any more than women should be submerged by men's terms.

Even if one were to grant, for the sake of argument, that we should embrace Mr. Mom as the best metaphor we have for liberating fathers, a fundamental question emerges. What, exactly, is "mom"? This is exactly the point Doucet raises in her critique of the question of whether men mother. As she writes, the question "carries the subversive implication that there is an 'ideal' kind of mother" (Doucet, 2006, p. 223). There is no ideal, Doucet tells us. Mothering is an ambiguous term informed by the "complexity and diversity of mothering in practice" (Doucet, 2006, p. 223). Some sort of definition is implied by the metaphor Mr. Mom. This term, after all, is applied to fathers who are acting like certain sorts of mothers. However, the phrase *certain sorts of mothers* indicates the problem. If there are certain sorts of mothers, then there are also other sorts. Which sort is Mr. Mom?

Some would say, pointing to the way in which the metaphor is used, that the father as Mr. Mom is nurturing. Mothers, after all, are the paradigms of the nurturing being. This interpretation is rooted, no doubt, in the fact of breastfeeding and in the cultural phenomenon of women as the family cooks. Nurturing, fundamentally, is linked to the verb *to nourish*. Women, as mothers, nourish their babies through breasts and bottles; they nourish their families through the meals they prepare. When the father becomes mother, he nurtures. This, surely, is the import of Piercy's breasted male: like women, he can breastfeed and thus nurture—nourish—the infant.

However, the link between mothering and nourishing as a necessary and unique activity is doubly problematic. First, as Simone de Beauvoir argues in *The Second Sex* (1989), woman as phenomenon is much more complex than we tend to think; surely mother is much more complex, as well. Beauvoir, for instance, reminds her readers that women have wombs, but are not determined by their wombs. Women have the ability to produce an egg, to allow that egg to be inseminated, and to nourish that growth of the inseminated egg within the uterus. Yet, women don't have to. They can't help but produce eggs (short of medical malady or menopause), but they don't have to procreate. Likewise, women don't have to use their breasts to nourish and don't have to cook meals for their families. Indeed, with modernity comes infant formula in a bottle: mothers, fathers, older sisters and brothers, and caretakers of all sorts can now nourish the infant by means of what is, essentially, a plastic and rubber breast. Mothers can and do share the responsibility of cooking with the men in their lives: fathers, like mothers, can cook. Not only can they bring home the bacon, they can fry it up, as well.

The link between mothering and nourishing as a necessary and unique activity is problematic for another reason. As Larry May argues in *Masculinity and Morality*, it is problematic because fathers as men are thus held to a minimum standard: the ability to provide semen in order to procreate. Mothers, as women, are held to a much higher standard: the ability—indeed, the responsibility—to nurture. This point echoes Doucet's criticism of the question Do men mother? As she writes, this question is problematic, in part, because it "holds women firmly to the moral responsibility that they will be primary caregivers of children" (Doucet, 2006, p. 223). This assumption belies the cultural reality that Doucet has studied: many men are acting as the primary caregivers. Further, it assumes as necessarily natural a cultural practice that is not necessarily natural: men can and do act as the primary caregivers of children. May argues that we need to "shift the burdens and benefits of nurturance and child care from the exclusive purview of women to include *male* child rearers" (May, 1998, pp. 38–39).

Why? May argues that one reason is that boys will pay a price when fathers don't nurture. What kind of men will these boys become when their only model of fathers includes what May and Robert Strikwerda call the "traditional" father (the disciplinarian who is involved with his children's lives only in order to enforce the law of the father), the augmented "traditional father" (more involved with domestic life but still allows the mother to nurture) or the sensitive new age guy (the dad who wants to be friend, not a father, to his children) (May and Strikwerda, 1996, p. 198)? Or, to use the metaphorical categories provided in this book: what kind of men will these boys become when their only models of fathers include deadbeats, thundergods, architects or fools?

7

Dad Incarnate

The parent who wakens and lovingly responds to the child's cries—or the parent whose embrace is sought by the sleepy child—is a metaphoric encapsulation of nurturing.

—Andrea Doucet, *Do Men Mother?*

Image

When my son was a toddler, I had a memorable conversation with a feminist Quaker mother. Her first child, a boy, was much older than my son. Hers was beginning to think about college. We were talking about feminism, and what she said has helped me in my own thinking about raising a boy: "It's our job to produce good husbands and fathers."

Mr. Mom is a metaphor that falls short of the mark. I believe that another metaphor is emerging in the North American cultural narrative, a metaphor that names these fathers who would act as liberating agents within the lives of their children: dad incarnate. Just as our cultural narrative explores, expands, promotes and nurtures the negative metaphors for father, it also has begun to offer this healthier alterative, albeit tentatively, marginally and uncertainly.

I have no doubt that my Quaker friend would fully agree with Larry May, author of *Masculinity and Morality*. Why should men nurture their children, especially their sons? Because to do otherwise is to produce men who can't provide nurturance: they will become, most likely, fathers who are not agents of liberation.

Larry May and Robert Strikwerda offer a strong argument for nurturance as the defining characteristic of the "good" father (and, indeed, the "good" mother). They "see nurturance as a complex, multi-level notion. To be a nurturer is 1) to display caring behavior for an extended period of time; 2) to have an intellectual commitment to that caring; 3) to identify oneself as a nurturing person" (1996, p. 197). They further argue that it has been difficult for fathers to see themselves as nurturers because of the link between nurturing and nourishing, because of the link between nourishing and the role of the mother (1996, p. 198). In order to free men to see themselves as nurturing fathers, May and Strikwerda rightly argue, we must understand the words *nurturing* and *nourishing* as metaphors. We do not need to read these words literally, linking nurturing to nourishing to breastfeeding and the provision of the primal meal.

This, I take it, is the import of the epigraph, drawn from Andrea Doucet's book, *Do Men Mother?* Doucet poetically claims, in the midst of sociological study of Canadian men who serve as the primary caregivers for their children, that "the parent who wakens and lovingly responds to the child's cries—or the parent whose embrace is sought by the sleepy child—is a metaphoric encapsulation of *nurturing* (Doucet, 2006, p. 111). Like May and Strikwerda, Doucet in this quotation is moving away from "mother" and "mothering" as the standard term by which we judge good parenting, and moving toward "nurturing" as the standard term. Further, she is uncoupling the apparent "necessary" link between "mother" and "nurture." As the epigraph beautifully imagines, metaphorically imagines, any parent—mother or father, male or female—can fill this role, can nurture the child.

Thus, when my daughter wakens me in the middle of the night by stroking my right ankle, which is sticking out from under the bed sheet, in order to be carried back to her bed, to be assured that the troubling dream was, indeed, only a dream, I am nurturing her, at least by Doucet's metaphoric standard. Am I mothering her? I would say no. Am I nurturing her? I would say yes: I cuddle her; I bear her back to the comfort of her bed, her head resting on my shoulder, her arms wrapped around my neck, her legs wrapped around my torso.

At this moment, I am not the deadbeat father, ignoring my child, leaving her to her mother's care. I am not the thundergod, yelling at her to return to bed. I am not the architect, hoping that my plans allow her to care for herself.

I am not the fool, stumbling as I take her back to bed, only to be rescued by wife. I am, rather, at least for a moment, a nurturing father, gently carrying my youngest—tender in the night—back to bed.

If we do stop at the literal meaning, it is difficult to argue that men should nurture, let alone are capable of nurturing. After all, if the mother is more closely linked to nurturing because of her physical ability to nourish through the womb and the breast, and her cultural role to nourish through the meal, then men, by negative definition, can't nurture. If nurturing is exclusively the province of women, and thus mothers, then it is not the province of men, and thus fathers. May and Strikwerda rightly remind us to realize that "to nurture" is a metaphor, and that the concept at the root of the metaphor is available to fathers. Cohen's study of 30 informants—fathers all—suggests that fathers themselves are beginning to embrace the idea that they too can nurture, that nurturance is not necessarily the unique activity of the mother. Cohen reports that most of the fathers he interviewed do not think of "providing" as their first duty. Rather, they spoke about "nurturing activities" as being their first duty (Cohen, 1993, p. 13). In contrast, Townsend's study of fathers tells us that fathers "said the most important thing they did for their children was to provide for them" (Townsend, 2002, p. 53). What is this concept at the root of the metaphor? "Sustained care including education and discipline, toward mature development" (May and Strikwerda, 1996, p. 198).

As I understand it, "mature development" for the human person is liberation: redemption and emancipation from the bonds and bindings that would limit our growth as free beings. In order to enter into this type of nurturing relationship with our children, fathers must incarnate themselves in the lives of their children. In other words, they must enter into their children's material beings; they must matter to their children. This understanding resonates with May's vision of true fatherhood: the "condition of being in a caring relationship with one's children through which one nurtures, supports, and educates them. Fatherhood ... is an accomplishment, not a simple matter of biological fact" (May, 1998, p. 30).

Gavanas (2002) provides a study of the Fatherhood Responsibility Movement. This movement, comprising in the main members of the religious right, also speaks of moving fatherhood beyond mere insemination and financial provision into areas of nurturance and care. As Gavanas details them, however, most rely on gender divisions that I reject, gender divisions that do not promote the liberation of children, fathers or mothers. For instance, one stream of the Fatherhood Responsibility Movement cautions the new nurturing father to maintain his hard masculinity, as opposed to his spouse's soft femininity: the father is to be the hard nurturer, the mother the soft one (Gavanas, 2002, pp. 213–242).

Dad incarnate, on the other hand, is a powerful metaphor that can help fathers of all stripes and persuasions find their way in a postmodern culture littered with deadbeats and thundergods, architects and fools. As dads incarnate, fathers enter into the particular material existence of their children. It is in this material relationship that dads can act as liberating agents, working to help their children to be free beings. One genius of postmodernity is that we have come to realize that the metaphors that were once bound to particular cultures and traditions have been opened to others. Just as many American poets looked to the cultures of Asia after World War II to help them find their poetic voices, just as many North Americans of European descent now read African-American and Aboriginal literature in order to help them discover themselves anew, just as many North Americans study Asian martial arts as ways of being in the world, I believe that the Christian metaphor of incarnation can help us name liberating fatherhood and liberating fathers.

The literature on the Christian idea of incarnation is vast. Crucial to the concept is the metaphor at its centre. To become incarnate is to take on carnal reality, to become body, embodied, flesh. This, of course, is the genius of the Christian narrative. The father God—distant, remote, powerful—realizes that he must enter into the carnal life of his creation in order to liberate it. As the creator father God, he created fleshly creatures, creatures of the earth. As the creator father God, however, he was necessarily not fleshly, not of the earth. The problem? There was a gulf between the two realities. The divine reality is fleshless, an ethereal existence separate from the fleshly existence that it created and cares for. The earthly existence is flesh-full: humans have bodies. Humans sweat, bleed and experience somatic and psychic joy and pain. The solution, according to the Christian doctrine of the incarnation, is for God to enter into human form, to become flesh and experience embodied pain and pleasure.

Referring to incarnation does not make this a book of theology or even a book for Christians only. The lesson to be learned is univeral: as fathers seek to act as liberating agents in the lives of their children, they, too, must become flesh, must enter into the material reality of their children's lives. This embodied father, this incarnate father, condemns the deadbeat, the thundergod, the architect, the fool. These inadequate and even harmful types of fathers do not enter as liberating agents into the carnal lives of their children, into the embodied reality that their children live. The deadbeat abandons the carnal reality, preferring to pretend that it doesn't exist. The thundergod stands apart from the carnal reality of children, issuing edicts and orders without experiencing, for himself, that carnal reality. The architect is fascinated by the carnal reality, tinkers with it, creates it, plans it, but does not live it. The fool lives it but is too bumbling to act as a liberating agent within it.

Once the father becomes dad incarnate, the cultural narrative is beginning to suggest, the father can act in a way that supports his children's growth toward freedom. He can act as a liberating agent, helping his children to find both redemption and emancipation.

This argument runs counter to the contention Allan Bloom forcefully presented in his 1986 bestseller *The Closing of the American Mind: How Higher Education Has Failed Democracy and Impoverished the Souls of Today's Students*. Bloom argues that men can be taught to "care," but this age project is doomed to failure (Bloom, 1986, pp. 129–130). Why? First, we live in the era of individualism. When the individual is the standard, why will individuals care about others? They will, first and foremost, care about themselves. Bloom suggests that this era presents a problem to women as well as men. Why will women care about others when they see their individual selves as the most important aspect of their existence? Second, if one is to care, one can care only about what one "possesses." If women, in the age of feminism, claim that they aren't the possessions of men, and if men come to believe this, then men cannot care about their women and the children they create with these women because they don't possess them.

I reject Bloom's argument for two reasons. First, I don't agree that we live in an era in which the individual is the standard. I see mothers and fathers and brothers and sisters and aunts and uncles and nieces and nephews constantly giving to each other. Second, I would argue that we can and should speak of belonging to each other rather than possession. We care when we realize that we belong, when we realize we are members of each other's lives, not when we possess.

Public Incarnation

One of the great tales of incarnate fatherhood in the North American cultural narrative is found in one of the most successful series of films in history: the Star Wars saga. (We have looked briefly at one film in the series, *Return of the Jedi*. Here we will look at the series as a whole.)

At the centre of all six films is Anakin Skywalker/Darth Vader—the fatherless child who, as an adult, fathers a son whom he is destined to liberate even as the son liberates him. The liberating action is not a private affair: it is played out as part of the destiny of a galaxy, the fate of billions of life forms hanging in the balance.

This film series—whose presence ranges from the films themselves to action figures to books and Lego, to devotees dressing like their favourite characters at screenings and other events—is entrenched in our culture. While many know the basic characters and narrative arc, I will summarize these for those who haven't seen all the films.

Anakin Skywalker is a young slave boy born of a virgin. The Jedi—mysterious and noble monastic devotees of the Force—decide that Anakin was born to "bring balance" to the Force,which has been teetering as of late, the "dark side" (that of evil and malicious intent) growing stronger.

Anakin is rescued from slavery and trained to be a Jedi.. But all is not right with him. He is aggressive, arrogant, jealous and a liar. A great Jedi fighter, he is seduced by the master of the "dark side" and becomes Darth Vader in order to save the life of his wife, who is pregnant.

Vader is a malevolent force. Together with the Emperor, he slays most of the Jedi. Of particular note is that Vader walks into the Jedi Temple and slaughters children who are training to become Jedi. A man who becomes evil so that his wife and, presumably, their child might prosper destroys a group of children whom he should protect. Already he is moving out of embodiment: he cares so little for the carnal existence of these relatively helpless children that he murders them without remorse.

All is not lost, however. Vader's wife gives birth to twins. The boy, Luke, becomes a Jedi, and learns that he must destroy Vader (not knowing that Vader is his father) in order to restore balance to the Force and thus liberate the oppressed creatures of the galaxy.

Luke, however, believes that there is good in Vader; Luke's final encounter with that good reveals the way in which the Star Wars movies are an important part of the North American cultural narrative's construction of the incarnate dad.

Years before, when Anakin had turned to the dark side, he lost both his legs and was badly burned. The Emperor found him and gave him new life, of a sort: Anakin emerged from reconstructive and prosthetic surgery as the black-robed Vader, more machine than man. He has already psychically left the realm of carnal reality; now he physically leaves it, as well. His own fleshly life cannot sustain itself: machines sustain him.

Vader is the ultimate deadbeat dad. He abandons his wife and unborn children.

When Luke confronts Vader, Luke refuses to fight him and tells Vader that he still senses good in him. Vader mournfully tells Luke that there is no good left, that he is fully part of the dark side of the Force. He takes Luke to meet the Emperor, who wants to turn Luke to the dark side, sensing in the son of Vader power greater than that which

Vader himself possesses. Even as he watches his rebel companions being led into a trap that will mean their death, Luke at first refuses to fight Vader or the Emperor, refuses to be drawn into angry revenge.

Finally he can hold back no longer. As Luke turns to strike the Emperor, Vader parries his son's light sabre and the duel between father and son begins. Luke's anger carries the day, and just as he is ready to kill Vader, he hears the Emperor urging him on, telling him to give in to his anger, to kill his father, to take his father's place at the side of the Emperor. Luke refuses, and throws down his light sabre, saving his father's life. The Emperor then decides to kill Luke; the young Jedi is too dangerous, too strong. As he is being attacked by the Emperor, Luke calls out to his father for help. Vader hesitates, looking from Emperor and master to son. He then grabs the Emperor and throws him to his death, becoming mortally wounded in the process. Luke wants to heal him, but Vader tells him it is too late. However, Vader tells Luke that he has already saved him. Vader's dying request is this: he wants Luke to remove the mask—a breathing and vision apparatus—that helps keep him alive. He wants to look at Luke, his son, with his own eyes. Luke does so; father and son gaze upon each other and then Vader dies.

Vader is a development of the metaphor of the incarnate dad because he chooses to enter into the carnal materiality of his son's life in order to liberate his son. This decision has a price: Vader himself dies.

His return to the material and mortal world, and thus his action to liberate Luke, comes, interestingly, only because

Luke acts as a liberating agent for his father. Luke refuses to believe that his father is pure evil. Luke's belief that his father still has good in him, Luke's refusal to kill his father, Luke's entreaty for his father's help: these redeem his father. This redemption allows Vader to act as a liberator in the fullest sense: he emancipates Luke by killing the Emperor and redeems Luke by acting as an emancipator.

Luke is provided with a model of incarnation: he can be like his father, a man who in the end is willing to sacrifice his own life for the liberation of his son's.

In a decidedly less cosmic way, Michael Dorris's memoir, *The Broken Cord*, reveals how the incarnate dad, acting as a liberating agent in the privacy of family life, touches and is touched by the public world. *The Broken Cord*, a National Book Award winner, is a painful and heroic story about Dorris's adoption of young boy and the subsequent discovery that the child has Fetal Alcohol Syndrome (FAS).

The story begins when Dorris, a professor of anthropology at Franconia College in New Hampshire, decides that he wants to be a father. Normally, this is not a particularly momentous decision, but Dorris is single and wants to adopt a Native American child. While working as an anthropologist in a remote Alaskan fishing village in 1971, Dorris had contemplated "improbable light, awhirl in the energy of star and sea. The colors above me and below merged incoherently, washed into each other and into me" (Dorris, 1989, p. 3). The result? Dorris's mind is "temporarily cleansed" and in the cleanliness he saw what he wanted: "I wanted a baby" (Dorris, 1989, p. 3).

This admission gets to the heart of Dorris's memoir, to the heart of the emergence of the metaphor of dad incarnate. Men may say, and indeed have said, that they would like a son, perhaps even a daughter. Few men in our culture would say, "I want a baby." This is the language of girls, of women, of mothers, be it the fruit of biology or environment or both. Try as we might, my wife and I were never able to get our son particularly interested in the dolls we bought for him when he was a toddler. My daughter, however, immediately gravitated toward babies: even as a little girl, she imagines herself to be a mother: she holds her babies, feeds her babies, dresses her babies, carries her babies. She even, on occasion, pretends to give birth by shoving one of her babies up her shirt and then helping it come out, head first.

So, when Dorris reports that he wanted a baby, he is moving into dangerous territory, a place where most men do not go: he longs for the province of the mother. As he himself says, single parenting was a "practical norm" in his family (Dorris, 1989, p. 3), but what was not the norm was single parenting by a father. His grandfathers and father had "died young, leaving widows to raise children alone and through extended family networks" (Dorris, 1989, p. 3). Dorris's "role models were strong, capable mothers, aunts, and grandmothers" (Dorris, 1989, p. 3). Already, then, as the memoir opens, Dorris names himself as a man who wants to venture into the territory of motherhood: he wants a baby and he wants to raise it as his own mother raised him.

He doesn't get a baby after all, but happily adopts a three-year-old Native American boy, whom he calls Adam.

Dorris doesn't care that Adam is the son of alcoholic parents, that Adam has been diagnosed as mildly retarded, that Adam has a limited vocabulary. He travels to South Dakota to meet Adam and bring him home. As they fall asleep together on their first night back in New Hampshire, Dorris asks, "How often in a four-day period can one person fall in love with another, each time as if it is the first?" (Dorris, 1989, p. 15).

This question, like his declaration that he wants a baby, shifts Dorris into the territory of the mother. Dorris is not a thundergod, an architect or a fool. He is, rather, a single man who wants a child and finds himself amazed at the depth of his love for this boy. It is as if Dorris has given birth to Adam and looks at him enraptured, as we so often see mothers (and paintings of mothers) looking at their babies. Dorris has moved into the material life of this boy and, as we come to discover, fully engages himself as a liberating agent on behalf of Adam and, because Adam has FAS, on behalf of other children with FAS.

The Broken Cord is a personal tale of Dorris's life with Adam and the people who join them to enlarge their family. (Dorris adopts two more children and then marries Louise Erdrich, a novelist, with whom he biologically fathers two children.) It is, at the same time, a professional tale of Dorris's research into FAS. As he and Adam live to together and love each other, it becomes clear to everyone that Adam has serious problems. As Erdrich says in her foreword to the memoir, it took Dorris months to teach Adam how to tie his shoes, and this was the least of Adam's problems (Dorris, 1989, p. xii).

The intersection of the personal and the professional—of the ways in which Dorris fathers Adam as an incarnate dad, of the ways in which Dorris attends to Adam both as his son and as a person with FAS, and thus as a metaphor for all children with FAS—is seen throughout the memoir, but perhaps nowhere better than the end. Dorris writes,

> My son will forever travel through a moonless night with only the roar of wind for company. Don't talk to him of mountains, of tropical beaches. Don't ask him to swoon at sunrises or marvel at the filter of light through the leaves. He's never had time for such things, and he does not believe in them. He may pass by them close enough to touch on either side, but his hands are stretched forward, grasping for balance instead of pleasure. He doesn't wonder where he came from, where he's going. He doesn't ask who he is, or why. Questions are a luxury, the province of those at a distance from the periodic shock of rain. Gravity pressed Adam so hard against reality that he doesn't feel the points at which he touches it. A drowning man is not separated from the lust for air by a bridge of thought—he is one with it—and my son, conceived and grown in an ethanol bath, lives each day in the act of drowning. For him there is no shore. (Dorris, 1989, p. 264)

Dorris, in this passage, sees Adam as who he is as Adam, what he can become as Adam. Dorris does not impose his own vision on his son, trying to mould him as he, the father, wishes him to be. This is an extraordinary effort, which places Adam's own freedom above Dorris's desire to have a particular kind of son, made in the image of the father.

Dorris is the type of person who does "swoon at sunrises" and "marvel at the filter of the light through the leaves." Recall the moment at which he knew that he wanted a baby. Dorris is the type of person who wonders where he comes from and where he's going. Adam is not. *The Broken Cord* is more than a tale of a son with FAS; it is, as well, a tale of a father who loves that son, who publicly shares his own journey as a father of that son.

Despite the many challenges, Dorris does not turn away from Adam, does not reject him. It would be tempting for a father to reject a child who disappoints him, who does not live up to his standard.

Dorris, however, commits himself to the son with whom he fell in love. This isn't to say that Dorris is without blemish. *The Broken Cord* is an honest book, revealing Dorris's frustration, anger and impatience. But it also shows a father who takes seriously the material reality of his son's life and acts as a liberating agent for and with that son. He seeks the best education for his son, medical help, job possibilities and, finally, acknowledges and accepts and embraces who his son is. This, perhaps, is the greatest act for freedom that any father can commit himself to. The son is not the father; the daughter is not the father. They are their own persons; the father who would be incarnate, who would live within and for the material reality of his children, knows this. As painful as it might be, his love and actions allow them to be free to be who they are: always connected to, but not—not ever—an image of the father.

Private Incarnation

If we see in *The Broken Cord* the incarnate dad who melds and mixes and merges the public and private worlds, we see in the 1979 film *Kramer vs. Kramer* a more private delineation of the possibilities of the incarnate dad. This claim is not without its detractors, from both the right and the left. The fact that *Kramer vs. Kramer* is the subject of derision from cultural interpreters who sit on opposite ends of the interpretive spectrum might, however, suggest that *Kramer vs. Kramer* is a point of discovery precisely where we can see the metaphor of dad incarnate beginning to emerge.

In chapter 3 we explored the idea of Kramer the father as metaphorical architect. He has constructed a family he does not inhabit. Kramer the mother, psychically crushed by her situation, decides to leave the marriage, abandoning husband and son.

Thus the movie begins with shock: the mother is the deadbeat; the father is left to care for child and house. At first, Mr. Kramer is pathetic, unable even to prepare breakfast for his son. He can't provide nourishment.

Things go from bad to worse until Mr. Kramer begins to realize that he wants to be an incarnate father more than he wants to be in advertising, fully immersed in professional life. He loses his high-powered job when it becomes apparent that he cannot single-mindedly pursue his career and live with the material world of his son's life. He ultimately finds a less-prestigious job that allows him to care for his son more intently and intentionally. In the movie, a new type of father unfolds before our eyes. Over time, father and son develop a profoundly close relationship: the father bathes his son, feeds his son, talks to his son, plays with his son.

Eventually, Mrs. Kramer returns, healthy and strong, and sues to establish her motherly role: she wants custody of the child. Mr. Kramer, newly incarnate in his son's life, also wants custody: he realizes that his own liberation as a human being comes from his life with his son and he believes that he has acted and can continue to act as a liberating agent in his son's life. Mr. Kramer loses the custody battle in court, but the movie ends with Mrs. Kramer doing the unthinkable: seeing that her ex-husband has grown and changed, she decides that their son, indeed, can find liberation by staying with his father.

For his part, Michael Kimmel, a left-leaning scholar, whose own sympathies lie with the general thesis of this present book, finds this movie to be problematic, both for men and for women. Kimmel argues that the film is "a modestly hopeful sign" for "a new vision of fatherhood" but it comes at a cost. First, it takes "an ironic slap at feminism. We were invited to cheer when his ex-wife ... finally decides to renounce her efforts to gain custody, since we have just witnessed the emergence of the sensitive new father from the chrysalis of an indifferent careerist. If put to the test, men turn out to actually be better 'mothers' than women" (Kimmel, 1996, p. 290).

Kimmel's interpretation is not unwarranted. *Kramer vs. Kramer* does present a vision of a failed mother who abandons her children, a tale nearly unthinkable in our culture. We do not have a phrase for women who abandon their children: there is no "deadbeat mom." Kramer the mother "finds herself" only by abandoning her family. This could be read as an implicit criticism of feminism, or at least feminism of a certain type. The film seems to suggest that women who want their own lives, who want a career, who want not to be trapped in a lonely existence need to walk away from their husband and children. If this is feminism, most North Americans could not do anything but criticize it.

However, another reading of the film, and its relationship to feminism, is possible. Mr. and Mrs. Kramer find themselves in a dialectical relationship that is set by a cultural pattern. He marries, impregnates his wife, provides money for them, and psychically abandons them to pursue his public life. She marries, is impregnated by her husband, and focuses on domestic concerns, eventually feeling trapped and destroyed by the situation.

How does she change it? Change him? Change culture? She needs her husband to become incarnate in the material life of the family, but can he do so without a radical change in the paradigm? This, of course, is Marge Piercy's point in the futuristic novel *Woman at the Edge of Time* that we explored in chapter 5. If culture is going to move into a better space, in which men as fathers, women as mothers, children as children are going to find freedom, the paradigm of family relationships must change. Women must give up the primal power of milk and blood, and men must give up their belief that women and only women can and should live within and for the material reality of their children. Is the resolution offered by *Kramer vs. Kramer* ideal? Certainly not. Is it, at its deepest centre, an attempt to help us all rethink the domestic economy so that we can begin to see the possibilities of the incarnate dad? I say yes.

Kimmel, however, also maintains that *Kramer vs. Kramer* is problematic because Kramer, as a man, finds his new masculinity in an area that is "so feminized." That is to say, Kimmel seems to think that men cannot find their new maleness as incarnate dads because this realm of domestic life, so long dominated by the power of milk and blood, is altogether too female. Kimmel argues that *Kramer vs. Kramer*, at its most fundamental level, is saying that Kramer the father is a better mother than Kramer the mother. Men cannot be men if they are pretending to be women, Kimmel seems to suggest. He writes, "This is an old theme, perhaps, but it still didn't work. Masculinity could not be reclaimed in an arena so feminized" (Kimmel, 1996, p. 290).

I agree with this last sentence, as my criticism of the metaphor of Mr. Mom shows. However, I fail to see how Kramer the father is acting as a mother, unless one accepts that the male incarnation into the life of the child is necessarily a feminization of the male. Why must this be so, except for the cultural practice that this role is a female role, and thus a motherly one? As Kimmel himself argues, definitions and practices of masculinity and, by extension, femininity, are culturally produced. It is true that the incarnation of fathers into the material lives of their children is dangerous because it implies that men are becoming women, that fathers are becoming mothers. I suggest that we stop seeing nurturing by fathers as a kind of mothering. This view of fathering is not only limiting, it is damaging. By sticking to this rigid interpretation, which is not a comfortable one for many men and women, we encourage fathers to turn to other metaphors or wander helplessly in the wasteland of metaphors we now inhabit. Both of these options are detrimental: to fathers, to mothers, and to their children.

My claim that *Kramer vs. Kramer* exemplifies the metaphor of dad incarnate, and the film itself, are criticized from the right, as well. Allan Bloom, in his infamous 1986 book *The Closing of the American Mind*, recoils at the thought that *Kramer vs. Kramer* has been seen as a helpful metaphorical guide. Referring to the names of the actors who played Kramer and Kramer, Bloom writes in horror that men are being led to believe that "they must accept the 'feminine elements' in their nature. A host of Dustin Hoffman and Meryl Streep types invade the schools, popular psychology, TV, and the movies, making the project respectable" (Bloom, 1986, p. 129).

Bloom accepts that any movement in the direction of what I am calling "incarnation" means, for men, feminization. Why, I must ask again, is nurturance distinctly and uniquely a feminine characteristic? Why is a father who makes a meal for his child seen as feminine? Why is a father who changes his child's diaper seen as feminine? Why is a father who takes his child to a playground seen as feminine? Why is a father who comforts his child in the middle of the night seen as feminine? Why is the father who kisses his child's scrape seen as feminine?

It is time for us to think in a new way, for us to realize that incarnation can mean for all of us a new world. In this world, we are free to act for the liberation of each other. This liberation is both redemptive and emancipating, allowing us to break free of the old ways of thinking about fatherhood.

Epilogue

Full liberation is rare, perhaps not even fully imaginable. After all, what is it to be redeemed fully? To be emancipated fully? Individual human lives are complex, to say the least. Always they are in development; always they must be seen in their particular contexts.

It is now well accepted, in the so-called Western world at least, that human life can be understood developmentally, as a process of stages. The infant is different from the toddler, who is different from the child, who is different from the adolescent, who is different from the young adult, who is different from the adult, who is different from the older adult. It is neither easy nor wise to generalize between these folk other than at the most abstract levels. Should their life trajectories be on the path of liberation? Without question. However, that is where the problem lies: what does liberation mean for a toddler? For a teenager?

Further, individuals cannot be understood apart from the contexts in which they live. Consider: a boy living on a farm in 2007 Iowa is different from a boy in living in town in 1907 Iowa, who is different from a woman living in a village in 2007 Nova Scotia, who is different from a woman living on a farm in 1907 Nova Scotia, who is different from a boy living on a farm in 2007 Iowa. What does liberation mean for the boy on the farm? For the woman in the village?

In light of this book, how must fathers act in order to serve as agents of liberation for their children and partners, even as these fathers recognize that they, their children and their partners live lives that are in development, that are located in particular contexts?

We can, I think, discern glimpses of liberation, of liberatory fathers who act as agents of liberation both for and with their children and the mothers of these children. To follow the *via negativa*, we know that such liberatory fathers certainly are not pedophiles. Neither are they any of the following metaphors that this book has explored: they are not deadbeats, not thundergods, not architects, not fools, not even, tempting as it may seem, "Mr. Moms." Each of these metaphors fails: some more so, some less so. The deadbeat fails because it is a metaphor of abandonment: children are left fatherless, left to struggle with and against the shadow, the trace, of the father who has left them intentionally. The thundergod and architect fail because they are, in their inverse relationship, inadequate. Both claim the child, unlike the deadbeat, but both fail: the thundergod pontificates without tenderness; the architect simply watches, taking notes. Dad as fool, while more tender and caring than either the thundergod or the architect, is an incompetent, depending on the mother to mother both him and his children. Mr. Mom, although better than these others, is problematic for number of reasons: it doesn't take seriously the fact that fathers are men. It reifies a particular understanding of women, and it does not consciously and carefully address the key component of parenting: the act of nurturing.

So what metaphor can we find in the *via positiva*? Liberatory fatherhood, I have suggested, is best seen in the metaphor of incarnation, of what I call "dad incarnate." Such a phrase is not meant to mimic traditional Christian understandings of the incarnation, thus reifying the gendered stereotype of the Father God becoming man, and thus, as feminists argue, making men, and fathers, into God. The phrase, however, may help us rethink not only human fathers, but also our image of the Father God itself. The phrase *dad incarnate* is meant to build upon the following question: What would it be for fathers to move into the particular material existences of their children in such a way that foremost in these fatherly minds, these fatherly hearts, these fatherly souls, is the desire for their children to be both redeemed and emancipated—to be, in short, liberated?

I also suggest, as two corollaries, that fathers themselves can find liberation in such incarnation, and that in their incarnate activities they also work as agents of liberation on behalf of the mothers of their children.

Liberated from what? Liberated for what? Here, we are brought back to the beginning of this epilogue. Liberation must be seen in context: liberation for the eighteen-year-old Jewish male living the life of bourgeois ease in Manhattan is, most likely, different than liberation for the five-year-old Mennonite female living a life of rural poverty in Ontario.

I offer the following two poems to end this book—two poems that might hint at liberation. Like many poems, they are tentative, limited, obtuse images. My eyes are still covered, waiting to be opened to the fullness of what might be if fathers dedicate themselves to the incarnate life of liberatory fatherhood.

Elias

I look and
see not
me my
eyes,
nose, nape
exposed but,
rather, flesh
incarnate.

What
a thought: is
he the
one this
baby born
of blood, body
opened?

My Children in the Garden

I dream of them both
naked in the plush
garden without

sense of loss, no need
for clothes. Feet simply
brushing purple

curving iris beards
tickling knees then thighs:
laughing my children

swirl, twirl not "ashes
we all fall down" but,
rather, bright stars.

Notes

1　Martin Luther King, *A Testament of Hope*, (1991, pp. 245–6).

2　My discussion of metaphor is drawn from my earlier book, *The Elements of Figurative Language* (Stull, 2001), and, as will become evident, Lakoff and Johnson's germinal work in the field, *Metaphors We Live By* (Lakoff and Johnson, 2003). The earliest explicit and systematic Western discussions of the nature and characteristics of metaphor appear in Aristotle's works, particularly *On Rhetoric* and *Poetics*. In *Poetics* (21.7), Aristotle defines *metaphor* as "a movement of an alien name either from genus to species or from species to genus or by analogy" (Cited in Artistotle, *On Rhetoric*, ed. George Kennedy, 222 n. 25).

3　Lakoff and Johnson add to this definition when they speak in terms of "domains" in order to distinguish metaphor from its sibling, metonymy (2003, p. 265). Lakoff and Johnson write, "In a *metaphor*, there are two domains: the target domain which is constituted by the immediate subject matter, and the source domain, in which important metaphorical reasoning takes place and that provides the source concepts used in that reasoning." About metonymy they write that "there is only one domain: the immediate subject matter. There is only one mapping: typically the metonymic source maps to the metonymic target ... so that one item in the domain can stand for the other." In other words, metaphor moves between language or conceptual domains. Metonymy does not. For instance, the word *dog* describes a being that belongs to the domain of non-human domestic animals. The word *father* describes a being that belongs to the domain of human animals, especially with reference to family. To say "that father is a dog" is to move from one domain—that of non-human domestic animals—to another—that of human animals, especially with reference to the family.

4 See Daniel Callahan's "Bioethics and Fatherhood" (1996) for an incisive discussion of this phenomenon from the viewpoint of philosophical ethics.

5 See Stull, 2001.

6 See David Tracy, *Plurality and Ambiguity* (1994). My discussion is indebted to his work. Also see my *Religious Dialectics of Pain and Imagination* (Stull, 1994) for my initial use of Tracy's ideas.

7 See Malcolm X, *The Autobiography of Malcolm X* (1965).

8 See Stull, *Religious Dialectics of Pain and Imagination* (1994) and Stull (1999) for fuller discussions of Freire, as well as the numerous books by Freire himself, including *Education for Critical Consciousness, Pedagogy of the Oppressed,* and *Pedagogy of the City.*

9 This is an instance of what Lakoff and Johnson call a spatial metaphor: it works within area (Lakoff and Johnson, 2003, pp. 14–21).

10 See Kimmel (1996, p. 249) for a very fine discussion of the film.

11 The comic strip *Beetle Bailey* offers another variation on this theme. General Halftrack, the commander of Camp Swampy, is at the mercy of his wife. Hagar, the fierce Viking of the comic strip *Hagar the Horrible,* rules the public sphere but is a buffoon at home.

12 See Gavanas (2002) for a cogent discussion of the Fatherhood Responsibility movement, for one example.

13 Also see LaRossa for a discussion of the economics of family life. He argues that the industrial revolution required fathers to leave home in order to earn a wage, leaving the mother in charge of the domestic sphere (LaRossa, 1997, pp. 26–27).

Bibliography

Amend, Bill. 1994. *May the Force Be with Us, Please: A Fox-Trot Collection.* Kansas City: Andrews McMeel.

———. 1997. *Come Closer, Roger, There's a Mosquito on Your Nose: A FoxTrot Collection.* Kansas City: Andrews McMeel.

———. 1998. *Welcome to Jasorassic Park: A FoxTrot Collection.* Kansas City: Andrews McMeel.

Aristotle. 1991. *On Rhetoric: A Theory of Civic Discourse.* Trans. George Kennedy. New York: Oxford University Press.

Austen, Jane. 2003. *Pride and Prejudice.* New York: Bantam.

Baldwin, James. 1952. *Go Tell It on the Mountain.* New York: Dell.

Berenstain, Stan and Jan. 1968. *The Bears' Vacation.* New York: Random House.

———. 1981. *The Berenstain Bears Go to the Doctor.* New York: Random House.

———. 1990. *Life with Papa*. New York: Random House.

Bloom Allan. 1986. *The Closing of the American Mind: How Higher Education Has Failed Democracy and Impoverished the Souls of Today's Students*. New York: Simon and Schuster.

Burke, Kenneth. 1961. *The Rhetoric of Religion*. Berkeley: University of California Press.

———. 1968. *A Grammar of Motives*. Berkeley: University of California Press.

Burnett, Frances Hodgson. 1998. *The Secret Garden*. New York: HarperTrophy.

Callahan, Daniel. 1996. "Bioethics and Fatherhood" in *Rethinking Masculinity: Philosophical Explorations in Light of Feminism*. 2nd ed. Larry May, Robert Strikwerda, Patrick Hopkins, eds. Lanham, MD: Rowman and Littlefield. 161–171.

Carr, Sr. Anne E. 1988. *Transforming Grace: Christian Tradition and Women's Experience*. San Francisco: Harper and Row.

Chopp, Rebecca S. 1989. *The Power to Speak: Feminism, Language, God*. New York: Crossroad.

Cohen, Theodore. 1993. "What do Fathers Provide? Reconsidering the Economic and Nurturant Dimensions of Men as Parents" in *Men, Work, and Family*. Jane C. Hood, ed. Newbury Park, CA: SAGE. 1–22.

Connell, R. W. 1995. *Masculinities*. Berkeley: University of California Press.

Daly, Mary. 1973. *Beyond God the Father: Toward a Philosophy of Women's Liberation*. Boston: Beacon Press.

de Beauvoir, Simone. 1989. *The Second Sex*. New York: Vintage.

Dorris, Michael. 1989. *The Broken Cord*. New York: HarperPerennial.

Doucet, Andrea. 2006. *Do Men Mother? Fathering, Care, and Domestic Responsibility*. Toronto: University of Toronto Press.

Eliot, George. 2003. *Daniel Deronda*. New York: Penguin Classics. Introduction by Terrence Cave.

Fiorenza, Elizabeth Schüssler. 1984. *Bread Not Stone: The Challenge of Feminist Biblical Interpretation*. Boston: Beacon Press.

Freire, Paulo. 1989. *Pedagogy of the Oppressed*. Trans. Myra Bergman Ramos. New York: Continuum.

———. 1990. *Education for Critical Consciousness*. Ed. and trans. Myra Bergman Ramos. New York: Continuum.

———. 1993. *Pedagogy of the City*. Trans. Donaldo Macedo. New York: Continuum.

Gavanas, Anna. 2002. "The Fatherhood Responsibility Movement: The Centrality of Marriage, Work, and Male Sexuality in Reconstructions of Masculinity and Fatherhood" in *Making Men into Fathers: Men, Masculinities and the Social Politics of Fatherhood*. Barbara Hobson, ed. Cambridge: Cambridge University Press. 213–242.

Gavison, Ruth. "Feminism and the Public/Private Distinction." Stanford Law Review, vol. 45, no. 1 (November 1992). 1–45.

Harrington, Daniel J., S.J. 1983. *The Gospel According to Matthew*. Collegeville, MN: The Liturgical Press.

Hawthorne, Nathaniel. 1992. *The Scarlet Letter*. New York: Wordsworth Classics.

Hearn, Jeff. "Men, Fathers, and the State: National and Global Relations" in *Making Men into Fathers: Men, Masculinities and the Social Politics of Fatherhood*. Barbara Hobson, ed. Cambridge: Cambridge University Press. 245–272.

Kimmel, Michael. 1996. *Manhood in America: A Cultural History*. New York: Free Press.

King, Martin Luther, Jr. 1991. *A Testament of Hope: The Essential Writings and Speeches of Martin Luther King, Jr.* Ed. James M. Washington. San Francisco: HarperSanFrancisco.

Jenkins, Philip. 1996. *Pedophiles and Priests: Anatomy of a Contemporary Crisis*. New York: Oxford University Press.

Lakoff, George and Mark Johnson. 2003. *Metaphors We Live By*. Chicago: University of Chicago Press.

Bibliography

Laqueur, Thomas W. 1996. "The Facts of Fatherhood" in *Rethinking Masculinity: Philosophical Explorations in Light of Feminism*. 2nd edition. Larry May, Robert Strikwerda, Patrick Hopkins, eds. Lanham, MD: Rowman and Littlefield. 173–190.

LaRossa, Ralph. 1997. *The Modernization of Fatherhood: A Social and Political History*. Chicago: University of Chicago Press.

Levertov, Denise. 1997. *The Stream and the Sapphire: Selected Poems on Religious Themes*. New York: New Directions.

Lewis, C. S. 2005. *The Lion, the Witch, and the Wardrobe*. New York: HarperCollins.

Malcolm X. 1965. *The Autobiography of Malcolm X*. New York: Ballantine.

Marx, Karl and Friedrich Engels. 1967. *The Communist Manifesto*. New York: Penguin.

May, Larry. 1998. *Masculinity and Morality*. Ithaca, NY: Cornell University Press.

May, Larry, and Robert A. Strikwerda. 1996. "Fatherhood and Nurturance" in *Rethinking Masculinity: Philosophical Explorations in Light of Feminism*. 2nd edition. Larry May, Robert Strikwerda, Patrick Hopkins, eds. Lanham, MD: Rowman and Littlefield. 193–210.

McFague, Sallie. 1987. *Models of God: Theology for an Ecological, Nuclear Age*. Philadelphia: Fortress.

Meier, John P. 1980. *Matthew*. Wilmington, DE: Michael Glazier.

Nix, Garth. 2003. *Mister Monday*. New York: Scholastic.

———. 2004. *Grim Tuesday*. New York: Scholastic.

———. 2006. *Drowned Wednesday*. New York: Scholastic.

———. 2006. *Sir Thursday*. New York: Scholastic.

———. 2007. *Lady Friday*. New York: Scholastic.

Ogden, Schubert. 1979. *Faith and Freedom: Toward a Theology of Liberation*. Nashville: Abingdon.

Piercy, Marge. 1976. *Woman at the Edge of Time*. New York: Ballantine.

Roethke, Theodore. 1975. "My Papa's Waltz." *The Collected Poems of Theodore Roethke*. New York: Anchor Press.

Rowling, J. K. 2003. *Harry Potter and the Goblet of Fire*. New York: Scholastic.

Ruether, Rosemary Radford. 1983. *Sexism and God-talk: Toward a Feminist Theology*. Boston: Beacon.

Sage, Angie. 2005. *Septimus Heap, Book One: Magyk*. New York: Katherine Tegen Books.

Saramago, Jose. 1994. *The Gospel According to Jesus Christ*. Trans. Giovanni Pontiero. New York: Harcourt Brace and Company.

Stull, Bradford T. 1994. *Religious Dialetics of Pain and Imagination*. Albany: State University of New York Press.

——. 1999. *Amid the Fall, Dreaming of Eden: Du Bois, King, Malcolm X and Emancipatory Composition*. Carbondale: Southern Illinois University Press.

——. 2001. *The Elements of Figurative Language*. New York: Longman.

Townsend, Nicholas. 2002. *The Package Deal: Marriage, Work and Fatherhood in Men's Lives*. Philadelphia: Temple University Press.

Tracy, David. 1994. *Plurality and Ambiguity: Hermeneutics, Religion, Hope*. Chicago: University of Chicago Press.

Weisner-Hanks, Merry E. 2001. *Gender in History*. Malden, MA: Blackwell.

Wiesel, Elie. 1960. *Night*. Trans. Stella Rodway. New York: Bantam.

Wilson Kastner, Patricia. 1983. *Faith, Feminism, and the Christ*. Philadelphia: Fortress.

Wood, Julia T. *Gendered Lives: Communication, Gender, and Culture*. Belmont, CA: Thomson/Wadsworth, 2003.

Wrede, Patricia C. 1993. *Talking to Dragons*. New York: Harcourt.